Teaching Modern Educational Dance

For Mrs Elizabeth Tiller
(née Gee),
formerly of Liverpool Education Committee,
with many thanks

Teaching Modern Educational Dance

Wendy Slater

Member of the Dance Specialist Team
for Liverpool Education Committee

Formerly Lecturer in Dance at
Ethel Wormald College of Education

Northcote House

Slater, Wendy
    Teaching modern educational dance. — 2nd ed.
    1. Modern dance — Study and teaching
    I. Title
    372.8'6   GV1753.5

    ISBN 0-7463-0372-6

© Wendy Slater

First published 1974, reprinted 1976 and 1979. This edition published in
1987 and reprinted in 1990 by Northcote House Publishers Ltd,
Plymbridge House, Estover Road, Plymouth PL6 7PZ, United Kingdom.
Tel: Plymouth (0752) 705251. Telex 45635. Fax (0752) 777603.

Printed in Great Britain by BPCC Wheatons Ltd, Exeter

Foreword

To those with little knowledge or experience in the field of educational dance it is perhaps necessary to enlarge a little on the purpose of teaching this subject in school.

Just as we communicate through the medium of the voice or the pen, so also can we communicate with our bodies through movement. Every gesture that we make, whether conscious or unconscious, is a means of helping to communicate something to others. When we say good-bye we often accompany our words with a shake of the hand. We may sometimes completely replace the spoken word with a movement, the most commonly used actions being the nod or shake of the head to indicate either "yes" or "no." A large part of a child's education is taken up by teaching him how to communicate his knowledge and his feelings. He learns to read, interpret and discuss what he has read. He learns to write and to pass on to others his own ideas on many subjects. In the creative dance lesson the child is learning to communicate through the medium of movement. Dance can be of especial value to the child who has difficulty in reading, writing and conversation. Those who are unable to read and write well are made aware of their own inabilities by their own ears and eyes. For a child who has creative energies it is most frustrating to be unable to communicate because of lack of these abilities. For these children dance is a release and a chance to be expressive without being measured against others. It is not necessary for the child to produce a series of superb movements as long as he has been able to express how he was feeling. After all, the child is unable to see himself as he moves.

Educational dance also provides opportunities to share creative experience with others. Children learn to adapt to each other and to lead in addition to sharing work in groups. This experience provides a basic training in relationships and a chance to explore the different social groupings that the children are to meet in adulthood.

When we view dance as a part of the physical education

programme it has a part to play in the training of the body by presenting opportunities to learn about the quality of movement. Gymnastics is also concerned with movement but in a more functional way, lacking the opening for self-expression and creativity on a more personal level. Each has an important role to play in the development of each child and in his education as a whole. Dance should not be seen as an isolated experience or even as simply a part of the physical education programme. It should be an integrated part of the school timetable linking with every aspect of education, both within the classroom and the environment.

Preface

THIS book is intended for all those who have an interest in and a basic knowledge of Modern Educational Dance but who find difficulty in the presentation of their material and the planning of the lesson. It should be of interest to mature students and teachers who have not had the opportunity of a lengthy course in dance but have, perhaps, attended short courses and now wish to follow up and gain additional knowledge through reading. For those students in training who are studying dance more comprehensively this book may be used as an additional source for creative ideas and as a guide to the development of the dance lesson in the Primary School.

Although the lessons included in the book are complete within themselves it is hoped that most teachers will use them only as a framework on which to build, with the needs of their own classes determining how they will progress. From these few ideas will grow other ideas stimulated perhaps by work in the classroom or from suggestions made by the children themselves.

I write in response to pleas from students and teachers who say that they either do not know how to begin or, having begun, do not know how to progress. I hope to have given these people the help and encouragement they need to fulfil their desire to teach Modern Educational Dance. It is to be hoped that as the teacher gains confidence so she will be able to build her lessons around her observation of her own children and to give ample scope in the lesson for the children's suggestions. Only in this way can they begin to develop a wide movement vocabulary and enable their movement experience to make a positive contribution towards their education as a whole.

W. S.

Acknowledgments

I AM very grateful to all those teachers and students who, by asking questions and showing an interest in my work, inspired me to write this book. I am also indebted to many Liverpool Primary School children without whom I should not have been able to produce the material for lessons I have suggested.

I should like to thank Miss Muriel Angus for typing this manuscript, and Mrs. Newman of the record department of Rushworth & Dreapers in Liverpool for her help in supplying reference numbers.

My thanks are also due to the following for permission to quote extracts from books: Evans Brothers for three poems from their "Book of a thousand poems"; Douglas Fraser for his poem "Small Creatures"; Bodley Head for the extract from the poem "Rejoice in the lamb"; Collins Press for the poem "In the swing"; Granada Publishing Co. for the poem "By the Sea"; William Heinemann for the poem "Slowly."

Contents

Contents

1
AN INTRODUCTION TO MOVEMENT

In the specimen lessons which occur later in the book the reader will note that the movement content of the lesson comes under the headings of main and subsidiary themes. I have given each of these themes a general title:

1. Body Awareness.
2. The Awareness of Space.
3. The Awareness of Weight and Time.
4. Relationship.

Taking each of these in turn, we will think about what each theme involves in terms of the dance lesson.

BODY AWARENESS

This theme concerns "what" is moving, and we begin by encouraging the child to use his whole body in each activity. Movements such as rising and sinking, spreading and curling, twisting and turning, can be introduced, and the children must be helped to include every part of the body in these activities. The teacher will find that the parts most often neglected are the head and the spine, and the children need constant reminders in the form of questions such as: "Is your head following the shape of the rest of your body?"; "If you are curled up, is your back rounded and your head tucked in as part of your small shape?"; "If you are making one side of your body important, perhaps your head could help by turning to look at that side," etc.

Young infants enjoy travelling around the room on their feet, so we must encourage them to use their feet in lots of different ways, *i.e.*:

hopping, skipping, running, jumping,
galloping, walking, leaping, etc.

In addition to using the feet in different ways, they may explore the possibilities of moving on different parts of the feet; the toes, the heels, the insides and outsides. Travelling activities can also be made more interesting by introducing size and exploring big and small movements.

From work on the feet we turn our attention to work with the hands, and children must be given the opportunity to discover how hands can shake, squeeze, spread, open and close, clap, rub one against the other—and how fingers can wriggle, meet and part, dance near to each other, around each other, and intertwine. The children will find that by using the hands to touch the floor in different ways thay can make different sound patterns. Hands can move near to the body and far from it, thus leading us into the next aspect of body awareness, which is elementary body shape. The body can be:

1. Wide or wall-like.
2. Tall or pin-like.
3. Small or ball-like.
4. Twisted or screw-like.

Children can explore these different shapes and enjoy moving from one to another, or moving along maintaining one of these shapes, or moving freely and choosing a shape to stop in.

In order to make the children aware of parts of the body other than hands and feet, they can be asked to dance making different parts of the body important. Knees in particular will play an important part in hopping and jumping activities, while the elbows can dance all around the body in different ways. The children will now be ready to begin small patterns of movement, *e.g.*

"I dance with my feet alone."
"I dance with my hands alone."
"I dance with my hands and feet together."

It is necessary for the teacher to use some sort of percussion accompaniment to help the children in changing from one to another. The teacher of the young infant will find that these aspects of "Body Awareness" will need constant repetition, and she will need to present the same material in a variety of different ways to give the children a sound movement basis upon which to build.

Juniors have a greater "movement memory" than infants and can create little patterns of movement and repeat them and their movement begins to have more form. They will not only work on the basic shapes but will also learn to differentiate between symmetric and asymmetric movements. The former emphasises both sides of the body equally, and the resulting movements are stable, controlled, and rather limiting. Asymmetry emphasises one side of the body, and is freer and more flowing and leads to all sorts of travelling and turning activities.

We progress from movements of isolated body parts to thinking about how different parts can be made more important as part of an activity of the whole body, and how eventually they can lead a movement. Knees and feet will obviously lead in travelling activities, whilst the hands and arms are the natural instruments for gesture which, in turn, leads to movement of the whole body. The chest is the centre of lightness in the body and is, therefore, instrumental in leading all sorts of rising movements and elevation. The pelvic area, being the centre of gravity, leads the body in strong downward activities.

Lastly, under the heading of "Body Awareness," we think of different body parts in contact with each other. Parts can actually have visible tactile contact, as in the case of the dance "Pat-a-cake Polka" (a national dance). Here the hands not only have contact with each other and the knees, but also touch the hands of another person. Contact, however, need not always be tactile. Parts of the body can meet and part, move around each other, interlink, etc. Work on this aspect can be a very good stimulus for partner work.

THE AWARENESS OF SPACE

Space can be divided into two main zones:

1. The personal space—otherwise known as the "kinesphere". This includes all the space immediately surrounding a person and is carried with him as he travels through the general space.

2. The general space. To reach this space necessitates

stepping or travelling as it involves that area of space which is outside the normal reach of the body.

Within the kinesphere, different parts of the body have their own areas of natural movement. Arms fill the upper area; legs fill the lower area. To reach out into zones which are not immediate, the participation of the centre of the body is necessary. This results in all sorts of bending, stretching and twisting activities. Gestures can either come from outside the body and travel in towards the centre, or begin in the centre and travel outwards. Hence we meet the two states of "near to" and "far from" the body.

Thinking in terms of the young infant, we are concerned first with encouraging him to use the general space and to travel using all the space, avoiding other members of the class. When the child has become proficient and gained confidence in this respect we would suggest that he finds other directions to travel in besides that of forwards. We are thinking in terms of the basic directions of backwards, forwards and sideways. It will be necessary to remind the children to look where they are going in order to avoid collisions.

Thinking again of the idea of "near to" and "far from" the body, the children are able to explore the space around the body seeing how far they can reach into the different directions—above, near to the ground, in front, behind, to the side. This exploration can be done by different parts of the body, forming a link with the theme "Body Awareness."

With juniors the work on the space aspect becomes more specific. Using the space around them the children will make air patterns that curve and twist. Pathways on the floor may now become wavy, curved, twisted or straight. Children need much practice in creating an angular pathway where straight lines are joined together with sharp turns.

We think also of the different levels in space—high, medium and low—and find different ways of moving, stressing each level. High level can be reached by stretching upwards on the toes and by all kinds of elevation. Medium level includes space on a level with the centre of the body, and requires movements which reach out in a horizontal manner. Low level can be experienced by kneeling, sitting and lying and by travelling keeping the body close to the floor.

Children can move from one level to another in different ways producing all manner of rising and sinking activities. Much of the progress occurs in relation to body awareness, and they have a growing awareness of the shape of the body in space. They learn also that space can be used in different ways, *i.e.*

1. By filling it—using all the limbs and constantly changing the focus from one place to another.

2. By exploring it—moving very carefully through the space.

3. By piercing it—perhaps by sharp jabbing, punching movements or by extending the body, or part of it, slowly through the space (*see* Table II, page 14 – last column).

There are many words that can help the children in the use of space. They can be used by the teacher as part of her dance vocabulary, or they may be used more specifically as the climax to a lesson when children perhaps try to interpret three or four words in movement while a partner observes and guesses the words.

THE AWARENESS OF WEIGHT AND TIME

We are thinking now about quality in movement. Having thought about which parts of the body are moving and "where" they are going in space we must turn our attention to "how" the body is going to move.

Weight qualities

1. Firmness—all movements which are strong and forceful and which require the participation of the centre of gravity. Teachers have a tendency to term strength in movement as "heavy." Heaviness is a lifeless, weightless attitude whereas firm touch involves the use of muscular tension.

2. Lightness—all movements which are light, delicate and give the body the feeling of being lifted through the air. Just as firmness requires help from the lower half of the body, so

lightness is helped by the chest, termed "the centre of levity," and emphasis is on movements that lift the body.

Time qualities

1. Suddenness—all movements which are quick, sharp, hurried and require sudden bursts of energy.
2. Sustainment—movements of a lingering, unhurried nature.

It is impossible to move in the style of one of these two qualities to the complete exclusion of the other, and therefore from the combination of the two grow the "weight-time" qualities. When we combine weight and time we have four new possibilities. They are: quick and light; quick and strong; slow and light; slow and strong.

(a) Quick and light—darting, quivering, flickering movements of a gay, lively nature.

(b) Quick and strong—sharp, energetic, vigorous movements.

(c) Slow and light—gentle, smooth, peaceful movements of a calm, quiet nature.

(d) Slow and strong—powerful, determined movements.

Infants are made aware first of all of variations in quick and slow movement. They may be asked to run as quickly as they can or to step with big, slow steps. Weight can be experienced by the gripping and releasing of the hands, and light, tiny steps contrasted with strong steps that "push a hole in the floor" or big, lively jumps. As children get older and have a wider vocabulary of movement, greater contrasts can be made, e.g. time can now be felt as a gradual change from one situation to another, or perhaps as a sharp, sudden change from one shape to another. Children will learn to make strong and light "statues" and to move in a strong or light dance in the space. Children at the junior stage who have a wide experience of dance may experiment with the weight and time combinations already mentioned, and will be helped greatly by the teacher if she uses percussion sounds to help stimulate and suggest the various qualities.

RELATIONSHIP

The term "relationship" is used to describe three different aspects. It can describe an individual relationship of one body part with another, either in stillness or while moving. It can also refer to the relationship of each individual child with the teacher or of one child with another child. Lastly, it might refer to the relatedness of one group of children to another in the dance situation. We have covered the first aspect to a certain extent under the section headed "Body Awareness." when body parts in contact were discussed. When we look at the second aspect we are thinking mainly in terms of partner and group work and of the different relationships children may achieve within this context.

The young child will have spent a great deal of time learning to be aware of his own body and how to adapt himself to the space surrounding him. Most of his awareness of other children will have been centred around learning to share the space with them and in avoiding them as he dances in the space. Now we wish to make the child aware that it is exciting to dance with other people and that things are possible in pairs or groups that are not possible when dancing alone. Partner work also gives opportunity for social training, and a chance for the child to learn that working with others means not always leading the way but sometimes adapting oneself to the ideas of other people. The teacher must create situations in which the child will have opportunity to share with other children, to lead movement, and to adapt and follow where other children lead.

The teacher can encourage the children to enjoy working with each other in several different ways, *e.g.*

1. "Doing the same", in which we aim to awaken the child's powers of observation. We may observe one of several ideas. For instance, the children may dance with the same quality—the movements will not necessarily be the same, but both children may be dancing in a strong, forceful manner; they may choose to dance in the same level—again the movements may not be identical, but both children may dance a little phrase in low level followed by a similar phrase in high level; the shape may be copied so that both children will finish in a similar shape—A may dance and

finish in a wide shape while B watches, and then B may dance and finish in an identically wide shape. Similarly, the children might choose to dance with an identical part of the body leading, or by copying a small rhythmic pattern.

2. "I go, you go", or the question and answer pattern. Here the movement of the first child has a direct bearing on the response of the second child. In "doing the same" the second child was learning to observe and copy. Here he is learning to observe and respond by doing something different. For instance, the first child may choose to do a high dance, using his hands to reach into the high places. The second child may reply by doing a low dance where his feet are most important.

3. "Dancing together." Having learnt to observe and copy, and observe and respond, we are now giving the child the opportunity to learn and share movement. This is much harder to achieve, and we need to help the children by suggesting various ways in which they might dance together without feeling that they need to dance in a very small area of space. The children can meet and part, pass by, travel around, avoid, touch, thus presenting many exciting possibilities for creating dances with the aid of ideas and suggestions from the teacher.

The desire to work and dance with one other person leads on to the idea of dancing in groups where a common idea might perhaps be shared. Groups might be small, perhaps trios or quartets, or on occasion the children might work together in larger groups. According to the number in the group different relationships will arise. A trio naturally suggests the two against one idea and more often than not extends into a dramatic idea in movement. The quartet can suggest a group of four, two couples, or the more dramatic idea of three and one. Larger groups suggest many possibilities in the change of relationships and of group shapes and formations.

Dancing with other people is a most important development in helping a child to adapt socially and to experience a variety of relationships with other people, and ample opportunity to explore these relationships must be given by the teacher.

2
PLANNING THE LESSON

In addition to the stimulus, each lesson must have a firm movement basis built upon the themes mentioned in Chapter One:

1. Body awareness and the instrumental use of the body.
2. Space awareness—level, direction, pathway, on the spot, travelling, near and far, etc.
3. Awareness of weight and time—strong and light, quick and slow, and combinations of the four.

In the general planning of the lesson one of these would be emphasised as the main theme and the other two would become subsidiary themes. This means that the concern would be, in the main, with one, but not to the complete exclusion of the other two. With young infants we generally emphasise the theme "Body Awareness" and are concerned with hands and feet, elbows and knees, and whole body movement. To give variety, however, we would still choose an aspect of space awareness and of weight and time as our subsidiary themes. With juniors, especially those who are not newcomers to dance, we might choose any of the three themes to be the most important. The one aspect which will be constant throughout each lesson will be that of "Relationship":

1. The relationship of the class and of each individual child with the teacher.
2. The relationship of one child with another.
3. The relationship within a group situation.

When we have chosen our movement content we turn next to the general structure and planning of the lesson. Each lesson should begin with an introductory activity. This is necessary for a number of reasons. It serves firstly to reawaken the children's awareness of the general space and to establish anew the relationship between the class and the teacher in the dance situation. The activity itself may not have any bearing on the theme of the lesson but be complete in itself. It may, on the other hand, be a revision of some movement aspect introduced in a previous lesson. It is usually some form of travelling activity, generally on the feet, *e.g.* skipping, galloping, running and jumping, etc. The teacher may suggest to the children a specific way of moving, and then encourage variety by reminding the children as they move of size, speed, direction, etc. On the other hand, the children might be asked to let their feet enjoy a dance all over the room, and from the teacher's observation the next idea may grow.

The second section of our lesson is known as the "Movement training." This is based directly on the main theme and includes all sorts of work on activities which are part of the climax. For instance, if the main theme is "Body Awareness," with special emphasis on hands and feet, the children will be led during the movement training to explore the many ways in which the hands and feet can dance (*see* Lesson One in the Infant series, page 44), although only one way may be used in the "climax."

The "climax" is the final part of the lesson and may either be complete in itself or a part of a longer dance idea that is continuing over a number of weeks. Most teachers complete their lesson with a small dance to a piece of music. It is by no means necessary always to use music for the "climax," as the reader will note when referring to the chapter on stimuli. On average, an infant lesson should last no longer than twenty minutes and a junior lesson no longer than thirty minutes. These times do not allow for the children to get ready for the lesson or to return to the classroom. This time should, ideally, be allowed for movement alone (*see* Table I, page 12, for time allotment).

THE TEACHER'S TASK

Although the teacher must have a good framework and a definite plan on which her lesson is based she must avoid the danger of dictating to the children the way in which they should move. Dance after all is a "creative" subject, and the children must be encouraged to explore all movement possibilities for themselves. The responsibility of the teacher is to ask the right question at the right time. If the children have been dancing with their feet and have all gone around in a circle, travelling only in a forward direction, the teacher must avoid the impulse to say, "Show me how you can go all over the room, travelling forwards, backwards and sideways." Instead, with suitable questions, she must encourage the children to find these directions for themselves, *e.g.* "I can see everybody travelling around the room following their noses. Could you find another part of the body to lead you a different way?" Here the children are not only exploring different directions in space but they are also being asked to think about which parts of the body are suitable for leading them in those directions.

The main task of the teacher in the dance lesson is to observe the children's efforts and to feed the children with ideas and suggestions which will encourage them still further. It is important, therefore, that the teacher does not take up a position in the hall from which she proceeds to teach the whole lesson but rather that she moves around the room seeing the movement from all angles and is able to comment and give help individually if necessary. If the children are to work in pairs or groups at any time during the lesson the teacher must be prepared to move among the groups giving ideas and suggestions and to show that she is interested in each group and not centring her attention on any one in particular. It is up to the teacher to make sure that children do not always choose to dance with the same partners or groups but that opportunity is given to exchange ideas with someone new. It has been said that the creative dance lesson should provide opportunity for "exploration, mastery and creativity." The task of the teacher, therefore, is to present a variety of material to her class in order that they may discover new possibilities, to observe and select material, and to enable the children to progress by clarification of movement to a greater mastery. We are not aiming in the school situation to produce great dancers, but we are hoping to stimulate the child to create something personal and original and to communicate through movement. It is important that the teacher is herself totally involved and cares about each child's creative attempts. She must know when to take active participation and when to withdraw from the situation.

"The lesson should aim to provide opportunities for the child to develop an understanding of his own movement capacities; to learn the language of movement and so invent and create sequences and dances of his own" (J. Russell—*Creative Dance in the Primary School*).

TABLE I

The lesson plan—30 minutes

⎰ Main theme: ⎱ Sub-themes:	One theme is emphasised to a greater extent, but certain aspects of the other themes will be covered in each lesson.	
Relationship:	Individual, pair or group.	
Accompaniment:	Possibly percussion, or short piece of music.	

		Timing
Stage One	*Introductory activity* Usually some form of travelling activity to re-awaken awareness of the general space and to establish a relationship with the teacher. Need not necessarily be centred on the main theme.	2–3 minutes
Stage Two	*Movement training* Based directly on the main theme and will also cover all aspects which are to be brought into the climax.	10–15 minutes
Stage Three	*Climax* Also based on the main theme. May be a pure movement idea or stimulated by a poem, music, sculpture, small story, etc.	10 minutes

The timing will vary according to the individual needs of the class.

3
STIMULI FOR DANCE

In any dance lesson we are aiming to get the children to move and respond freely to ideas given by the teacher. It is most important that movement should not be imitated but that it should be stimulated by a variety of means. There is an abundance of material from which we can draw to stimulate the child to dance. I have listed them in the chapter under four headings.

AURAL

Music: Music can be used to suggest changes of mood, to promote changes of quality, to suggest many different activities (*see* Chapter Four).

Percussion: Percussion sounds made on instruments or by the voice or hands can stimulate a variety of movements, or the shape of the instrument itself might suggest either a movement idea or a dramatic idea (*see* Chapter Five).

Words and language

When thinking of words in terms of movement they would seem to divide naturally into four main groups. The first group are nouns such as "wind," "machinery," "fireworks," etc., all of which suggest different types of movement. "Wind" can suggest gentle movements that lift and fall when we think of a breeze; a sudden movement that travels to a new place when we think of a "gust of wind"; continuous energetic movement using a lot of space when we think of a "gale"; turning, spinning, rushing, etc., when we think of a whirlwind. There are many nouns like this which suggest contrasting movement ideas. The second group of words I have called "descriptive sensation." These are words like "hot," "cold," "gay," "brisk," etc., which immediately suggest particular types of movement to convey the meaning in a moment. One might shiver to convey cold and move with sharp, sudden movements to suggest heat. The group of words we use most in the average dance lesson are those called "descriptive action" words like "whirl," "pounce," "hover," "dart," etc. These words describe particular movements rather than suggesting sensation.

TABLE II

Word Stimuli

Nouns	Descriptive "Sensation"	Descriptive "Action"	Mood words	Space words
Wind	Warm	Flying	Anger—Peace	Onto
Sea	Old	Whirling	Storm—Calm	Into
Machinery	Young	Pouncing	Sorrow—Joy	Over
Fireworks	Gay	Hovering	Hate—Love	Under
Elements	Leisurely	Creeping	Fear—Bravery	Around
Rain	Hot	Dangling	Caring—Indifference	Across
Thunder	Cold	Bursting	Death—Life	Through
Lightning	Sharp	Shooting		Above
	Hurried	Sprawling		Beneath
	Lively	Darting		
	Dull	Whirling		
	Strong	Falling		
	Gentle	Rising		
		Crawling		
		Spinning		
		Tossing		
		Drifting		
		Twirling		
		Gliding		
		Exploding		

Children can build small sequences of movement by choosing three or four of these words to build on.

The last group of words are probably the most interesting and stimulating because they suggest mood and emotion. These include words like "anger" and "pain." "Anger" can be shown in movement in many different ways. "Pain" can be sudden and gone or long and lingering. It can also be shown in terms of grief. Some of these words need no sound or accompaniment to help convey the meaning. "Fear" can be clearly shown in movement alone. These words might be used by older children as a starting point for dance drama. Children might, alternatively, work in pairs, each choosing a contrasting word. Words like "anger" can be helped by making vocal sounds to accompany the various movements.

Table II lists words under these headings, but the teacher will think of many more to add to those already suggested.

Story ideas

There are many books written to-day for the younger child which include a wide variety of stories. These offer a wealth of movement material for the teacher of dance if she selects and chooses carefully. Stories often include descriptions of characters, and this gives children an opportunity to experiment with characterisation. For instance, we might find that one of the characters is an "old man." Here the children can enjoy finding out what types of movement can signify "old age." In these cases the stories will be the starting point for the lesson.

Sometimes, however, the teacher may wish to work on a particular movement idea but would like to add to the interest by using a small story for the climax which is based on these ideas. Here it will probably be easier for her to create her own stories. Later on in the book there are several examples of how this can be done.

If we look in the Bible we also find another wonderful book of stories, many of which can easily be retold in dance. In the Old Testament are stories such as the Creation, the flight from Egypt, the story of Ruth, or Noah's Ark, and many more. In the New Testament there are stories such as the Nativity, the Easter story, the Temptations, some of the Parables. As some of these stories require a greater degree of understanding they will possibly be more suitable for the teachers of older children.

Stories may be the starting point for a movement idea which can develop in an entirely different way, or the aim may be to tell out the story with movements, thus using it both as the stimulus and as the climax to the lesson.

Poetry

Poems can be used for dance in the same way as a story. In fact, many poems actually tell a story. This poem, for instance, tells a story and yet suggests a very simple movement idea.

A Tragic Story

There lived a sage in days of yore,
And he a handsome pigtail wore:
But wondered much and sorrowed more
Because it hung behind him.

He mused upon this curious case,
And swore he'd change the pigtail's place,
And have it hanging at his face,
Not dangling there behind him.

Says he, "The mystery I've found—
"I'll turn me round"—he turned him round;
But still it hung behind him.

Then round and round, and out and in,
All day the puzzled sage did spin:
In vain—it mattered not a pin—
The pigtail hung behind him.

And right and left, and round about,
And up and down, and in and out,
He turned; but still the pigtail stout
Hung steadily behind him.

And though his efforts never slack,
And though he twist, and twirl, and tack,
Alas! still faithful to his back
The pigtail hangs behind him.

W. M. Thackeray.

This poem suggests a use of space with changes of direction and level and pathway. It actually leads into the movement idea rather than stimulating the child to tell out the story. This next poem, however, tells a story which can be re-enacted in movement.

Through Nurseryland

Now, rocking horse! rocking horse! where shall we go?
The world's such a very big place, you must know,
That to see all its wonders, the wise-acres say,
'Twould take us together a year and a day.

Suppose we first gallop to Banbury Cross,
To visit that lady upon a white horse,
And see if it's true that her fingers and toes
Make beautiful music wherever she goes.

Then knock at the door of the Old Woman's shoe,
And ask if her wonderful house is on view,
And peep at the children all tucked up in bed,
And beg for a taste of the broth without bread.

On poor Humpty-Dumpty we'll certainly call,
Perhaps we might help him to get back on his wall;
Spare two or three minutes to comfort the Kits
Who've been kept without pie for losing their mits.

A rush to Jack Horner's, then down a steep hill,
Not over and over, like poor Jack and Jill!
So, rocking horse! rocking horse! scamper away,
Or we'll never get back in a year and a day.

Anonymous.

The first verse suggests a rocking movement. The teacher
might work on rocking on the feet, both backwards and forwards, or sideways. Children can experiment with rocking on
different body parts. Verse two suggests a galloping activity
using all the space (visiting different places), followed by
lighter movements of fingers and feet on the spot (rings on her
fingers and toes). Verse three begins with the more mimetic
movement of knocking with the fists on an imaginary door
followed by quiet, gentle stepping about the room so as not to
wake the children. Verse four has a contrast in quality beginning with strong lifting, pulling or pushing movements and
continuing with gentle gestures of the hands and possibly feet
to suggest stroking. The last verse returns to the galloping
activity.

Some poems tell of particular characters and stimulate movement peculiar to this character, e.g.

Jack Frost in the Garden

Jack Frost was in the garden;
I saw him there at dawn;
He was dancing round the bushes
And prancing on the lawn.
He had a cloak of silver,
A hat all shimm'ring white,
A wand of glittering stardust
And shoes of sunbeam light.

Jack Frost was in the garden
When I went out to play;
He nipped my toes and fingers
And quickly ran away.
I chased him round the wood shed,
But oh! I'm sad to say
That though I chased him everywhere
He simply wouldn't stay.

Jack Frost was in the garden:
But now I'd like to know
Where I can find him hiding:
I've hunted high and low—
I've lost his cloak of silver,
His hat all shimm'ring white,
His wand of glittering stardust,
His shoes of sunbeam light.

John P. Smeeton.

The poem itself does not say how Jack Frost moves, but by reading it to the children one can set them thinking about Jack Frost—what sort of person he is and what he does to us. The result might be a little dance based on jerky, spiky movements of different body parts as Jack Frost dances high and low and all about freezing everything in sight. (See Appendix II for more suggestions of poems for movement).

Sounds

As well as percussion sounds there are many sound effects which can be used as the starting point for dance. In addition, there is the comparatively new medium of "electronic sounds" which can often be used most successfully to stimulate dramatic dance ideas and to create an atmosphere. The teacher can encourage the children to find their own way of creating sounds and sound patterns and help them to include and develop these in a dance situation.

VISUAL

Art

We are thinking here in terms of pictures or paintings, some of which may be of a scene which tells a story which again can be re-enacted in movement.

To-day many painters are concerned with shape and design, and paintings of this nature can lead to movement experience through the awareness of space and space patterns. Contemporary art can often suggest different things to different people, and a painting shown to children can stimulate them individually to create small dances based on their own interpretation.

It is possible for children and teachers to create their own designs from a particular aspect of movement, and then to use these designs as a starting point for movement.

We can take the basic space patterns, curved, angular, twisted, linear, and use them to make a design. By varying the thickness of the lines we draw we can suggest changes of quality within the pattern shown in Fig. 1.

This simple design can obviously be interpreted in many different ways, according to what each individual sees when he looks at it. It might suggest:

1. Travelling in a curving pathway, perhaps beginning slowly and increasing in speed to lead into—
2. an upward thrusting jump, and
3. a lighter landing followed by

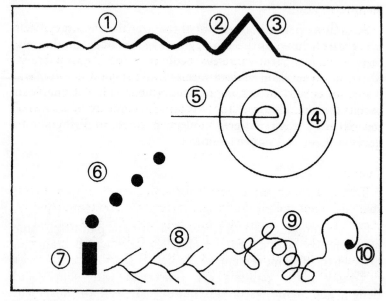

Fig. I

4. a curve that leads into a spiral movement on the spot with the body gradually closing again, opening into

5. an advancing glide with a pause followed by

6. four quick sharp movements (maybe punches into space or four angular movements with different body parts), finishing with

7. a strong direct movement, perhaps a downward press to low level, and then a contrasting

8. curving pattern, perhaps gesturing, accenting one side of the body and then the other while rising and travelling, culminating in

9. a twisting pattern on the spot, using all body parts, and ending in

10. a curved shape.

This may seem rather complicated but, in fact, children will enjoy creating their own designs and then interpreting them in movement.

Sculpture

Sculpture is a similar medium to that of painting, except that being three dimensional it can also suggest body shapes and can be an excellent stimulus to partner and group work. Shape in objects and sculpture might also suggest quality: *e.g.* a smooth curved object might suggest a movement gentle in quality and rounded in shape; a sculpture made up of a series of straight lines might suggest movement direct and angular in quality.

Colour

This is a much more personal medium, and I have found that although colour indicates variety of mood and quality there are no set examples one can use. Colours appeal to people in different ways and perhaps reflect their own personality. I have tried to suggest here how colours might be linked with different qualities:

> Red—for danger. Will suggest strength and speed. A fiery mood.
> Yellow—warm, like the sun. Flowing, lively, happy.
> Black—dark, funereal. Strong and slow. Sombre.
> Green—the sea. Neither strong nor light, quick nor slow. Twisted, billowing.
> Blue—cold and ice. Sharp, sudden, spiky, short-tempered.
> White—peaceful, calm. Gentle, unhurried. Pictures of snow.
> Purple—stately, graceful. Controlled, direct, dimensional.

TACTILE

Material

Different textures will automatically suggest different types of movement. Silk might suggest gentle movement of a flowing, undulating nature, while lace can suggest delicate, dabbing, fine touch gestures. Velvet is thicker and richer and might suggest a stronger, fuller movement.

Objects

There is a never-ending variety of objects which can be used, not only as visual aids but which can also stimulate a child to movement by their very feel. If we take the example of a sea shell, for instance, we can find sea shells which are rough and knobbly and feel spiky to the touch. In contrast we can feel a sea shell which is smooth and clear. The touch of these two can help the children to achieve a contrast between "spiky" and "smooth" movement. Similarly, they may appreciate the difference between "heavy" and "light" by holding first a large stone and then a feather.

ENVIRONMENTAL

In this section we look at the world about us. Many of the nouns suggested under word stimuli are also applicable here.

1. The elements—earth, air, fire, water, suggesting changes of effort and a varying use of space.

2. Machinery—exploring curves and angles, wheels and pistons.

3. The sea—waves, boats, playing on the beach, sea creatures, rock formations.

4. The sky—birds, aeroplanes, balloons, clouds.

5. Nature—the animal world, trees, plants.

6. Weather—thunder, lightning, wind, rain, frost, snow, ice.

7. The street—the people we meet like the postman, road-sweeper, park attendant.

8. Space—moonwalks, astronauts, strange planets.

9. Circus—animals, characters.

10. Occupations and working actions—hammering, sawing, digging, sweeping, bed-making, etc.

There are many, many more. These are only a few ideas to help the teacher to create interesting and varied situations in the dance lesson and to enable the children to differentiate between what is good and what is bad. It will awaken their appreciation of various media and should give them the opportunity to create and experiment for themselves. Although teachers will find that they have their own preference when it comes to choosing stimuli, it is important that a good balance is kept and that certain stimuli are not over-used to the exclusion of others.

THE LINK WITH THE CLASSROOM

It is hoped that the dance lesson will be an integrated part of the school curriculum. If this is so, there will be many occasions when things that happen in the classroom might suggest ideas for the dance lesson. Similarly, there are times when ideas explored in movement can be followed up by work in the classroom in a variety of subjects. Sometimes the link will only be with one other subject, but on occasion an idea in movement can be the beginnings of a topic involving many different aspects of education.

Poetry lessons can often be a means of stimulating movement ideas. On the other hand, events of the dance lesson can be a means of introducing children to writing their own poetry. Later in the book the reader will find a series of dance lessons based on the movements of a number of circus characters. It is rather sad to find that many children never visit a live circus, but most have had the opportunity to see the circus on television. Although one catches the thrill of the high trapeze or the tight-rope walker, the excitement can only ever be that of the watcher and never of the participant. In the dance the children have the opportunity of feeling what it must be like to move like a tight-rope walker or to juggle expertly. They will have read poems about these characters, but now, having had the movement experience, they may be able to write their own poems describing what it feels like to be part of the circus. We can see the possibilities of the same link with creative writing, when stories or descriptions the children have written can often spark off an idea for movement. On occasion we may not create a whole dance from these ideas but might use movement as a means of understanding the feelings of a character who has been introduced in one of the poems or stories. In this way we link the two facets of dance and drama in characterisation. Those children who have difficulty in communicating with words, either spoken or written, may find that they are able to communicate the same ideas through movement.

Sometimes the children become so excited by the dances they have created that they want to recapture their experience in some visual form. They might choose to draw a picture of their dance. If the dance was based on pattern they might choose to capture their own patterns by creating designs on paper. Work done in the ordinary art lessons can often produce excellent material for dance interpretation.

Recently a certain amount of research has been done into the possibilities of linking dance with religious education. By dancing the stories and great events of the Bible the children will not only come to a greater understanding of the meaning of them but might also be introduced to the greater experience of learning to understand and care for their fellow men. So often children are unable to identify themselves with the characters in the Bible when they read about them or hear them spoken of, and if opportunity is given to interpret these in dance children will come to realise the reality of situations which arose in the Bible and which are linked so closely with events to-day. Out of this experience should grow a desire for discussion and questions, not only on Biblical topics but also on topical events.

It can be seen that the work done in the classroom creates its own situations where a link may be made with the dance lesson. It is not necessary to contrive these situations. They can occur not only in the aspects already mentioned but also in history, geography, music and every other aspect of the school curriculum. It is the task of the teacher to take the opportunities when they arise and use them to enrich the experience and understanding of the child.

4
CHOOSING
AND INTERPRETING MUSIC

IT is most important that the music chosen for the dance lesson is appropriate for the theme, and also that it is used well. Those teachers who are fortunate enough to have a pianist to play for their lessons will be able to rely on both set pieces of music and on improvisation. Quite often one cannot foresee exactly how a dance is going to develop, and on such an occasion to be able to add improvised music after the dance has been created is ideal. The children will have been given ample opportunity to develop their own ideas without being tied down to a set musical pattern.

Unfortunately, the majority of teachers do not have the benefit of a pianist but must rely on the use of "canned" music. This is music which has been pre-recorded, either on record or tape. Although not providing the freedom of improvisation, the use of pre-recorded music also has advantages. It is obviously possible to ensure that the quality of the music is of a high standard. One is also sure that repetition is exact each time the music is used.

We can choose a piece of music to dance to without any preconceived idea of how to develop the movement. Here the music is the dominant factor and the movement becomes dependent upon it. This is good from the musical standpoint as it is not likely to be adjusted to suit the movement idea. Music can often be used in this way to stimulate the children to move freely at the beginning of a dance lesson, but I would not recommend building an entire dance lesson in this way except in the case of extremely gifted teachers who are able to build and develop the reactions of the children without any preconceived ideas of their own.

Alternatively, we can work out a scheme of movement and then try to find a piece of music which is suitable as an accompaniment. This method presents many problems as it is extremely rare to find a piece of music that exactly suits a plan. In desperation many teachers will begin to extract parts of music from different sources and join them together in an effort to make them fit the theme. This is not a practice to be recommended at all. Children should be encouraged to appreciate that music has a value of its own, apart from as an accompaniment to dance. In many cases the dance teacher will be introducing the children to music which they may not hear on any other occasion and, therefore, is certain to influence their appreciation. It is important, then, that music is chosen carefully and used in an appropriate manner.

It seems obvious that some form of compromise is needed if both music and movement are to be interpreted sensitively. It is necessary to have a general scheme of movement prepared but not planned out to the last minute detail. In this way it is generally possible to find a piece of music that is appropriate, and then to adapt one's own ideas so that music and movement can be brought together to create a satisfying whole.

Depending upon the theme of the lesson we will be looking for different qualities in the music. R. M. Thackray gives a comprehensive list of these qualities in the book *Music and Physical Education*—"rhythmic vitality, contrast of mood, clarity of phrasing, easily recognisable tunes, colourful orchestration, a strong emotional dramatic or atmospheric content . . . simplicity and immediate appeal to the ear. . . ." With the primary school child in mind I would add to this list the necessity of choosing short pieces of music which can be used on several occasions, so that the child begins to learn them and experiences a sense of security when moving to them.

Most of us have our own personal preference when it comes to choosing music, and there is a danger that we might overload the child with pieces of music all biased in the same direction. The teacher must aim, therefore, to introduce the child to a variety of music ranging from current tunes of the "pop" variety to the classical idiom. Popular tunes can often be used to accompany the introductory activity of your lesson. Chosen carefully, some of them have strong rhythmical patterns which suggest all sorts of travelling activities most suitable for re-awakening use of space at the beginning of the lesson. Here we might either suggest the activity ourselves or ask the children to "dance with their feet," leaving them free to interpret the music in their own way. On some occasions we may find a piece of pop music that suggests to us a particular idea and can be used a little more specifically in the "climax" of the lesson. Pop music used in this way is more suitable for older juniors, and an example of how an idea can be developed in this way is given in a later chapter, when I have used the Leroy Anderson tune *Syncopated clock* as a stimulus and accompaniment for a dance based on the movements of machinery. However, with most children hearing so much pop music elsewhere, I would suggest that it be used sparingly in this context.

Young infants respond very quickly to the old nursery rhymes. These again are rhythmical tunes and most suitable for starting the lesson. Many nursery rhymes suggest a skipping rhythm, *e.g. Nuts in May, Here we go round the mulberry bush, Pop goes the weasel*, etc. These tunes are also very clearly and simply phrased and provide an excellent introduction for the child.

When we come to choosing music for the movement training or climax we may be looking for something that suggests a change in quality. This may necessitate using two short pieces of music with contrasting qualities. If the chosen theme was "strong and light," we might choose a vigorous, dynamic piece of music with lots of bass, and contrast this with a slow, lilting tune, perhaps played on flute or quiet piano. For teachers who do not have access to a large record library this might sound rather daunting. Fortunately, there are quite a number of records now recorded especially for modern educational dance, and it is usually possible to find suitable music on these for the infant and lower junior age groups. For the top junior age group it may be necessary to look further afield to find exciting music which will stimulate the older child and maintain his interest. Boys in particular enjoy dance with a more dramatic bias, and there are many longer pieces of classical music which are most suitable for suggesting mood or accompanying a particular dramatic idea. Dukas's *The Sorcerer's Apprentice*, Stravinsky's *Rite of Spring*, Berlioz's *Symphonie Fantastique*, Saint Säens *Danse Macabre*, all present a mood of mystery and witchiness, while music like Debussy's *La Mer*, Mendelssohn's *Hebrides Overture* and Britten's *Sea Interludes* might suggest contrasting ideas of the sea.

On many occasions the dance teacher is not able to find exactly what she wants but has to be satisfied with second best. How frustrating it is to hear something on the wireless at a later date which is exactly what one had been wanting. It is clearly advisable for the teacher to make her own catalogue of suitable pieces of music and accompanying movement ideas for reference at a later date. It would not be possible to buy every record that one ever hears, but most towns now have a record library where for an annual subscription fee one may borrow records for a short time. Some suggestions for starting a record library for dance are given in Appendix III at the end of this book.

REPRODUCING YOUR SOUND

Nothing can be worse than choosing your music and planning your lesson and then having your lesson spoiled by a faulty record player or tape recorder. If music is going to be reproduced adequately it is necessary to care both for the records or tapes used and for the equipment. Remember that both records and tapes need cleaning. Ideally, records should be cleaned before placing on the turntable and again before replacing in the sleeve. Tapes do not need cleaning as frequently, but are inclined to lose the quality of sound eventually if neglected.

Many lessons can be spoiled if the teacher is not familiar with the use of the record player and tape recorder. The following are points of organisation, but the success of your lesson may hinge on whether or not you have noted them:

1. Make sure on the day of your lesson that the record player is actually working. In schools where only one record player is available and is used by a variety of people, it is quite common to find that it has "broken down." If this should happen to you, you will still have time to re-think the end of your lesson.

2. Check that you are using the right needle and are

playing your record at the right speed. Failure to do so could result in damage to the record.

3. Check beforehand on the volume needed to reach to the furthest end of the hall without distorting the sound. It is essential that every child should be able to hear the music clearly.

4. When using a record with several bands, take care that you do not scratch the record when placing and removing the needle from inner bands.

If you are not sure of your ability to begin the music in the right place, or if you are intending to use more than one piece of music in the same lesson, then it is wiser to use a tape recorder, and these points should be noted:

1. Music taped on a two track tape recorder can be replayed on either a two track or a four track machine. Music recorded on a four track tape recorder should be replayed only on a four track machine. In this way, if replaying music recorded on tracks one and two, one precludes the possibility of sounds from tracks three and four being reproduced at the same time.

2. Check before playing that you are running the tape recorder at the right speed for the recording.

3. Note the number at the beginning of your piece of music, so that should you wish to repeat it you can return the tape to the right place immediately.

Whether using a record player or a tape recorder, always check that the instrument is fitted with the right plug for the power point in the hall or room you are going to use.

5
THE USE OF PERCUSSION SOUNDS

WE have already discussed the possibilities of using music as an accompaniment and stimulus in the movement lesson. This chapter will look into the realm of sound, which is so much a part of our everyday life. Most daily actions are accompanied by their own sound patterns. When we walk down the street our feet make their own rhythmic sound; when we breathe we make a sighing sound. Sound accompanies so much of our activity that we tend to take it for granted.

Sound plays a very important part in the dance lesson, especially in the education of young children. They will respond particularly to sounds made by the teacher's voice. The voice can be particularly expressive when used to stimulate different qualities in movement, and can also create a variety of sounds other than words. Young children enjoy using their own voices, either to accompany their own movement or to stimulate others to dance. The body itself is also capable of creating percussive sounds either by making contact with the floor or by the meeting of two body parts. Hands can beat the floor; knuckles can rap; fingertips click; feet stamp, etc. Hands can clap one against the other, rub each other making a slithery sound, shake making a fluttery sound, etc.

As a means of accompaniment percussion instruments prove themselves invaluable. It is possible to play very simple rhythms on percussion—rhythms that are not embellished by harmony and that are easily understood, especially by the young child.

There are many percussion instruments which can be used, including tambours, tambourines, castanets maracas, bells, and cymbals. A full list of instruments and modes of playing are given in Appendix II at the end of the book. Instruments fit into three rough groupings:

1. Those which shake or vibrate, including shakers, sleigh-bells, castanets, tambourines and maracas.

2. Those which make a more melodic sound—including chime bars, cymbals, Chinese bells, xylophones, etc.

3. Those which we beat in order to create a rhythm, including tambours, drums, wooden blocks, sound sticks, etc.

All these instruments can be played to create rhythmic patterns, but each instrument is capable of making a particular quality of sound and is, therefore, likely to stimulate different qualities in movement. Certain instruments like the Chinese bells and xylophone have a light, delicate quality as contrasted with the stronger, shorter sound created by beating a tambour or drum. Understandably, one instrument from each group might be chosen to accompany or stimulate movement in a strong and light theme. A cymbal and a chime bar both make sounds that linger and gradually die away, whilst castanets and sound sticks make short, sharp, staccato sounds. These instruments would be suitable for accompanying movement, contrasting suddenness with sustainment.

Some instruments can be played to produce more than one quality of sound, the tambourine being the most notable of these. Having both skin and bells, it is possible to make a rhythmic sound by beating on it with the hand or a vibratory sound by shaking it. It is also possible to create a scraping sound by drawing the fingers or the nails across the skin. In particular the tambourine is invaluable for accompanying a variety of activities, especially travelling activities on the feet. All these activities have their own rhythm if you listen to the sound of the feet on the floor. It is important for the accompaniment on the tambourine to bring out this natural rhythm. The children will respond to these rhythms and feel more confident in the activity and it is, therefore, important to give them a framework of regular phrasing. If you are accompanying a skipping activity and have difficulty in playing it correctly, think of the nursery rhyme *Pop goes the weasel*. Skipping is the basic rhythm of this tune, and it is an excellent guide to the phrasing. If accompanying an activity like running and jumping, try to make the phrase for running the same length each time you play it. There is nothing more confusing for the children than not knowing when to jump. In Table III at the end of the chapter I have tried to suggest suitable accompaniments for a variety of activities.

Although the teacher will generally use some sort of percussive sound for accompaniment during the lesson, it is to be hoped that opportunity will be given for the children to play the instruments as well. When the children have explored the instruments and discovered the variety of sounds they can make they will be able to accompany their own movement patterns, either by finding a sound that matches the rhythm of the action or by trying to match the quality. From this they might progress to work in twos, one playing the instrument for the other. Older children enjoy working in larger groups with one or more instruments perhaps having contrasting qualities of sound.

Not many schools are fortunate enough to have a collection of percussion instruments large enough for each child in the class to have the use of one. Even those who have are not always willing to have expensive and sometimes delicate instruments used in this context. It is quite easy for the children to make their own percussion instruments in the classroom with only the need for a few easily collectable items. Simple shakers can be made by filling a tin or a plastic bottle with small stones, or by joining two yoghourt cartons together with sticky tape, having placed inside them an adequate amount of dried rice or dried peas. By varying the amount put in the shaker it will be found that the depth of the sound changes. Handbells can be made by making a hole in metal bottle tops and threading them onto wire twisted or joined to make a handle. It is also possible to make a fairly adequate cymbal by punching a hole in the centre of a large tin lid, threading cord through and knotting it underneath, and using a stick with which to beat it.

With a little ingenuity a large variety of instruments are quickly made, and children take great pleasure not only in making them but in being able to use them for their dance lessons.

Children are aware of rhythms from a very early age, and will respond readily to rhythmic phrases whether played on a percussion instrument or as part of a piece of music. They do not at first appreciate the quality of sound, but they will soon begin to understand that sounds do vary, some demanding response in a strong movement, some suggesting lightness and delicacy, etc. Percussion sounds, therefore, are not only valuable as a link with the musical education of the child but also as a link with the growth and understanding of the language of movement.

TABLE III

Activity	Instrument	Accompaniment
Walking	Tambourine	Continuous light beating with knuckles on the skin. Vary speed to change size and speed of step.
Running	Tambourine	Very quick, light beats of tambourine on the heel of the other hand.
Hopping, jumping	Tambour Tambourine Wooden block	Short, sharp, staccato beats either with knuckles or beating stick.
Running and jumping	Tambourine	Short phrase of shaking leading into a loud bang, followed by a smaller bang or slight pause to allow for landing. Shaking might gradually crescendo to suggest gaining speed to lift in the jump.
Skipping and galloping	Tambourine	Think of *Pop goes the weasel*. A rhythm of —— . —— . —— . —— . played by beating the tambourine with the knuckles.
Going and stopping	Tambourine	Short phrases of continuous shaking intersected by a pause held long enough to establish a stopping position.
Creeping, sliding, slithering	Tambourine	A scraping sound made either with a wire brush or by brushing skin with finger tips or nails.
Rising and sinking	Tambourine or maracas	A short, vibratory phrase beginning softly and rising to a crescendo. Pause. A short phrase beginning loudly and getting softer to sink to nothing.
Opening and closing; Gathering and scattering	Tambourine	These activities fit naturally into a $\frac{3}{4}$ rhythm. Beat tambourine lightly in waltz time accenting first beat slightly to emphasise one side—the other side.
Strong and slow	Large cymbal or gong	Loud, slow beats not allowing the sound to die completely away between each beat.
Strong and quick	Drum or tambour	Loud, sharp beats played continuously to suggest a thrusting action.
Light and slow	Chinese bells or high-pitched chime bars	Single light beats letting the sound die completely away between each beat.
Light and quick	Triangle	Holding metal beater at an inside angle of the triangle, make it vibrate very quickly from one side to the other.
Spikiness	Castanets	Short, sharp action of the wrist producing a sudden staccato sound.
Smoothness	Chinese bells or high-pitched chime bars	As for light and slow movement.
Turning	Tambourine or maracas	Continuous shaking of instruments.

6
SOME SUGGESTED LESSONS WITH PURE MOVEMENT STIMULI

THE following lessons are all based on various aspects of movement showing the development of the movement idea without the added stimuli of stories, poems, etc. The "climax" in most of these lessons is accompanied by a short piece of music. The lessons are not connected with each other and are not intended as a series but rather as individual lessons on a theme perhaps to be used as "starters," further work on each theme being planned by the teacher as a result of her observations.

HANDS AND FEET

Main theme: Body awareness, with emphasis on movements of the hands and feet.

Sub-theme: Space awareness—movements that travel using all the space; movements on the spot exploring the space around the body.

Relationship: Dancing alone.

Introductory activity

Let your feet take you on a dance all over the room. Perhaps you can sometimes dance on both feet and sometimes on one foot on its own.

Movement training

1. Can you do a skipping dance to the tambourine? Let me see your feet taking you high and low and all about.

2. Let your feet take you walking all over the room. Can you sometimes reach out with big, giant steps and sometimes dance in a tiny space with very small steps?

3. Keep your feet very still and let your hands make a

clapping noise all around you. How many different places can your hands reach into?

Sitting

4. Can your hands make a very loud noise around you on the floor? Can you make a different noise with another part of your hands?

5. Show me how your finger-tips can do a quiet, gentle dance on the floor.

6. Can your fingers dance in the air, sometimes moving very near to your feet and sometimes dancing far away from them?

Climax

Listen to the music. Show me how your feet and fingers can dance together around the room. Let them sometimes dance near to each other and sometimes far apart.

Music: *Nimble*, Listen and Move No. 4 (Green Label).

ELBOWS AND KNEES

Main theme: Body awareness with elbows and knees leading the movement.

Sub-theme: Space awareness—changes of level with rising, sinking and travelling.

Relationship: Dancing alone or partner work.

Introductory activity

Skipping all over the room making your knees very important. Can your knees lead you skipping in different directions?

Movement training

1. Show me a very high shape where your elbows are important. Can you do a high dance all over the room with your elbows reaching up to the ceiling?

2. Straighten your knees and make them very stiff. Can you walk with stiff knees? (Remember all the different directions—backwards, sideways, etc.).

3. Can you find another way to dance with your knees still stiff? (Skip, jump, etc.).

4. This time bend your knees until you are close to the floor. Can you do a very low dance?

5. Make a small shape. Choose one elbow and let me see how it can stretch and grow until it has stretched your whole body into a big shape. (Repeat several times, encouraging the children to find different ways to let the elbows lead the body, *e.g.* smooth, spiky, curving, turning, etc.).

6. When you have grown to be big show me how your knees and elbows can lead you dancing up and down and all around to stop in a shape with elbows and knees important when the tambourine stops.

7. Let your elbow draw you in again until you become a small shape once more.

Climax

No music. Small percussion phrases played by the teacher for rising with elbows leading, travelling with elbows and knees important, sinking with elbows leading. The teacher might repeat the pattern several times suggesting that the children find a different way of growing each time. Older children might work in pairs, one playing the percussion sounds for the other, and vice versa.

BASIC BODY SHAPES

Main theme: Body awareness with emphasis on the body shapes—wide, small, tall and twisted.

Sub-themes: Awareness of space—changes of level, going and stopping.

Relationship: Dancing alone.

Introductory activity

Skipping all over the room making every part of the body a part of the activity.

Movement training

1. Running and jumping. Explore and see how many shapes you can make in the air.

2. Small phrases of travelling and stopping. Choose a shape to stop in. Can you be very still in your shape? Is every bit of you a part of your shape?

3. Sitting: Show me how you can make your hands into different shapes. Can they be sometimes very wide and flat, sometimes very long and thin, sometimes squeezed into a small, tight ball, and sometimes very twisted?

4. Can you change your hands very slowly from one shape to the other? Watch them carefully. When I say "stop" I wonder if I can guess the shape they are in.

5. Make a small shape on the floor. Choose to be either wide, tall or twisted. Can you grow and grow until you have made the shape you have chosen. If you have chosen wide, are you as stretched as can be—reaching out towards the walls? If you have chosen tall, are you reaching up to the ceiling with your finger-tips and heads lifted high? If you have chosen twisted, are you screwed around with each part of you twisted in a different direction?

6. Can you stay in your shape and dance a wide, tall or twisted dance all over the room?

Climax

Listen to the music. Think about which shape you are going to choose. See if you can grow and dance to the music. When it stops let me see you very still in the shape you have chosen. (Children should have been encouraged and given opportunity during the movement training to have danced in all the shapes. In the climax they will probably choose the one they have enjoyed doing most).

Music: *Clitter clatter music*, Listen and Move No. 2 (Green Label)

ON THE SPOT AND TRAVELLING

Main theme: Space awareness emphasising using a small space and using all the space in the room. Using the three levels.
Sub-theme: Body awareness emphasising different body parts.

Relationship: Partner work.

Introductory activity

Walk all over the room thinking about change of direction, change of level, what part of the foot you are walking on. Emphasis on using the space properly.

Movement training

1. Skipping all over the room trying to get the whole body to participate in the skip.

2. Running with quick, lively steps travelling in and out of other class members.

3. Sitting with hands tucked in close to the body. Let them stretch out slowly into space and return very quickly and vice versa. (Teacher to accompany with percussion or voice. Encourage children to reach into a different area of space each time).

4. Curl up in a small shape. Let just one hand shoot out suddenly and come back slowly. Choose another part of you and let it shoot out somewhere else. Can two parts shoot out together?

5. Run and choose a new spot on the floor. Can you dance just on this spot, reaching into all the spaces? Dance right away from it and back to it again (small phrase on tambourine repeated several times).

Climax

Choose a partner and both of you go together and choose a new space. Beginning close together, one hold a shape while the other person dances around him on the spot and is still. The second person dances on the spot and is still. Both dance right away from each other and then back to the spot. Both dance together on the spot, *e.g.* "I go, you go. We travel together. We dance together on the spot". One of the couple might choose to dance making hands and feet important, while the other dances making elbows and knees important. One may influence the other so that they match each other at the end. Levels could be varied. No music. Teacher to repeat small percussion phrases used for movement training.

STRONG AND LIGHT (emphasising strong)

Main theme: Awareness of weight and time—quick and strong contrasted with slow and light movement.

Sub-theme: Body awareness with emphasis on feet and hands.

Relationship: Dancing alone.

Introductory activity

Skipping with very big skips letting your knees lift you as high as you can go. Can you do your big skips in lots of different directions?

Movement training

1. Skipping with little tiny skips that only take you a little way.

2. Listen to the tambourine playing sometimes for big skips and sometimes for little ones. Can you dance and match the sound on the tambourine?

3. Sitting: Can you make a very light dance in the space around you with your fingers? What sort of pattern can you make in the air? Try to watch your fingers wherever they go.

4. Let your fingers and feet join together to do a light, quiet dance all over the room. Feet so light that they do not make a sound on the floor.

5. Show me a very strong shape (knees bent, gripping the floor firmly with the feet). With strong fists let your hands punch all around you in the space—up to the ceiling, out to the sides, down to the floor, etc.

6. Walking with big strong steps, knees that shoot out in all directions (strong and direct).

Climax

Listen to the music. Show me a very strong starting shape. Can you make every bit of you strong as you dance about the room (strong feet, strong fists punching all around in the space)? See if you can stop in a strong shape when the music finishes.

Music: From *Appalachian Spring*, Copland: Listen, Move and Dance No. 2 (H.M.V.)—music for strong movement.

STRONG AND LIGHT (emphasising lightness)

Main theme: Awareness of weight and time, emphasising quick, light movement.

Sub-theme: Body awareness with emphasis on hands and feet.

Relationship: Dancing alone.

Introductory activity

Running all over the room on the toes with emphasis on use of space and quiet feet.

Movement training

1. Stepping about the room with loud, heavy steps as if "stamping in puddles" (picture image).

2. Stepping, again lifting the knees high but this time putting the feet down carefully and quietly.

3. Running with strong, lively steps, stopping still when the tambourine stops.

Sitting

4. Let your finger-tips do a light tapping dance all around you on the floor. Perhaps they can sometimes dance in the same direction and sometimes go different ways.

5. Let your hands make a very loud noise on the floor.

6. Can they make a loud noise against each other in the air?

7. Touch the air with your finger-tips, exploring the space all around your body.

8. Standing on the spot. Touch the floor with little light movements of the feet (first one foot and then the other).

9. Can you travel all over the room with quick, light steps that make a pointy pattern on the floor?

Climax

Listen to the music. Dancing with quick, light steps and

fingers that touch the air in a light, delicate dance all around you (emphasise change of direction and dancing high and low).

Music: *Quivery*, Listen and Move No. 3 (Green Label).

SPIKY AND SMOOTH

Main theme: Awareness of weight and time with emphasis on sharp, sudden movement.

Sub-themes   (*i*) Body awareness—emphasis on different body parts. Spiky shapes.

(*ii*) Space awareness—rising and sinking in different ways.

Relationship: Dancing alone.

Introductory activity

Skipping in and out of everyone else. Can you make different parts of your feet important?

Movement training

1. Walking all over the floor shooting your feet out in different directions, *e.g.* heels that shoot up behind you, toes that shoot out in front, sides of the feet that shoot across you, etc.

2. Can you walk very smoothly and quietly as if you were trying to creep past somebody without waking them?

3. Sitting: Fingers that make a gentle curving dance all around the body.

4. Make fingers, wrists, elbows into a spiky shape. Can you make a jerky, spiky dance with these parts of the body?

5. Make a shape near to the floor. Can your fingers, wrists and elbows lead you to grow in a spiky way? (Short, sharp beats on the tambourine).

6. Can you do a spiky dance all over the room? Do not forget feet, head, shoulders and all the sharp, angular parts of the body.

Climax

Children beginning in a group around the teacher. Travelling away from the teacher with smooth, gentle steps and fingers that make a curving pattern in the air (teacher to play gentle shaking rhythm on tambourine). When tambourine stops, children stop in a space in a curved shape. When music starts let one part of the body begin to move in a jerky, spiky way. Let the rest of the body join in until you are travelling all over the room in a jerky, spiky dance stopping in a spiky shape when the music finishes.

Music: *Mechanical Doll*, Listen and Move No. 4 (Green Label)

7
SERIES OF LESSONS FOR YOUNG INFANTS

THE following lessons are intended for a class which has not previously done any dance. The lessons are not intended as isolated sessions but are linked together as a series, each one arising as a result of the previous lesson. It is hoped that the material will be used as a guide to the teacher with the needs of her own class dictating her approach.

LESSON ONE

Main theme: Body awareness with emphasis on work with the hands and feet.

Sub-theme: Space awareness involving movement on the spot and travelling.

Relationship: At this stage the children are learning to be aware of the space and of their relationship with the teacher and are consequently dancing alone.

Introductory activity

Walking around the room using all the space. (Work on frequent changes of direction and introduce the ideas of moving, not only forwards all the time but sometimes backwards, sideways or round and round. Use a simple beating rhythm on the tambourine as an accompaniment.)

Movement training

Feet

1. Exploring the possibilities of moving on other parts of the feet, *e.g.* sides, heels, etc.

2. Discovering how many different ways there are of using the feet to travel around the room.

44

3. Make the feet dance on the spot and then contrast this by making the feet travel all over the room making a pattern on the floor, *e.g.* hopping, skipping, jumping, etc.

4. Choose just one way of dancing with the feet, *e.g.* skipping. Work at skipping with tiny skips only using a very small space. Contrast this with large energetic skips which travel all over the room using a lot of space.

Hands

1. Hands which clap and make a loud noise contrasted with hands that clap gently making no noise.

2. Hands which shake not only right in front of the body but in the spaces all around the body.

3. Rubbing the hands one against the other. Feel each part of the hand rubbing against every other part.

4. Fists that open and close perhaps slowly or quickly.

5. Hands that meet and part and turn around each other making patterns in the air.

6. Fingers that wriggle and skip in the spaces around the body.

Climax

Working individually using the idea of "I travel around the room with skipping feet. I stop still and make my hands move, dancing and skipping around my body. I make my feet and hands skip and dance together as I travel all around the room."

Music: *Boy and girl dance* from "Listen and Move No. 2,"
Side B (Green Label).

Teaching points

1. At this early stage in space training the children will need help in finding a space of their own in which they can move freely without coming into contact with any other child when moving on the spot and without colliding when travelling.

2. Encourage the children to explore different pathways as they travel around the room. If you suggest making different patterns on the floor this will stop the children from travelling round and round the room in a circular pathway.

3. The children will probably move in a forwards direction all the time unless encouraged to do otherwise. Whatever you do, do not dictate the way in which they move but let them discover the different ways for themselves.

4. In any activity which involves using the space around the body try to encourage the children to extend into all the space in order that the whole body begins to take part in the activity and will bend and straighten and twist and turn.

LESSON TWO

Main theme: Body awareness with emphasis on work with hands and feet.
Sub-theme: Space awareness with movement both on the spot and with travelling; going and stopping.
Relationship: Dancing alone.

Introductory activity

Running and jumping all over the room. Think about stretching in the air and landing on the toes.

Movement training

1. Running with small steps all over the room. (Short percussion phrases for going and stopping. Encourage stillness as soon as the tambourine stops playing.)

2. Stepping from one space to another sometimes very high up on the toes and sometimes low down near to the floor.

3. Skipping using all the spaces. Make the feet very important.

Sitting

1. Wriggle the fingers. Feel each finger moving on its own.

2. Clap the hands very loudly together and then gently making no noise at all. Do the same with the hands clapping the floor all around the body.

3. Rub the hands together and shake them.

4. Using the fingertips, do a skipping dance all around you on the floor.

5. Let the fingers skip all around the body using the space

above, below, in front, behind, far away, near to, at the side, etc.

Climax

With percussion accompaniment play a lively phrase for feet which skip all over the room followed by a quieter phrase of equal length for fingers which skip all around the body on the spot. Lastly, a vigorous, livelier sound for fingers and feet which skip at the same time as the body travels around the room.

Music: use again the small piece of music from the previous lesson called *Boy and girl dance*. This music has three distinct phrases suggesting the different movements and the children will be able to recognise them quite clearly.

Teaching points

1. When using the theme "going and stopping," make the stillness an active one. It should be a continuation of the previous activity and a preparation for the one that is to follow.

2. If using a percussion accompaniment always make sure that you phrase your sound and that your phrases are of equal length each time you play them.

3. In order to get total absorption in an activity where the focus is on the hands, always encourage the children to watch their own hands rather than watching you.

4. If working on stepping, or in fact any other travelling activity on the feet, with an emphasis on low level, always encourage the children to bend from the knees rather than from the waist.

LESSON THREE

Main theme: Body awareness with emphasis on work with the hands and feet.
Sub-theme: Space awareness—movement on the spot and travelling.
Relationship: Dancing alone.

Introductory activity

Can the feet dance around the room in lots of different ways? Perhaps they can make a pattern in the air as they dance.

Movement training

1. Can the feet dance with tiny movements on the spot and with big lively movements all over the room? (Use a quiet sound on the tambourine for movements on the spot and a louder sound for movements that travel.)

2. With the feet together do a little jumping dance all over the room. What sort of pattern can you make on the floor as you go? (Suggest directions other than forwards all the time.)

Sitting

1. Let the fingers do a dance all around the body.

2. Can they dance sometimes right away from the body so that the arms are stretched far away from each other and then back to the body and dance very close to it?

3. Wriggle the fingers and then the toes.

4. Clap the hands together. Can you find a way of clapping the feet together?

5. Let the hands do a shaking dance all around the body.

Standing

Can you shake each foot in turn in the space near to the floor?

Climax

During the movement training you will have been accompanying the various movements with different percussion sounds. Now choose three rhythms and three different ways of moving the hands to these sounds, *e.g.*

Clapping hands	accompanied by a steady beat on the tambourine.
Shaking hands	accompanied by a continuous shaking sound on the tambourine.

Skipping, dancing fingers   accompanied by a light skipping rhythm on the tambourine.

Work on phrases of travelling making the feet dance. Accompany this with a lively travelling rhythm on the tambourine. When this sound on the tambourine stops begin to play one of the chosen rhythms for work with the hands and let the children join in on the spot with the movement that matches the sound. You will find that the children are quite able to recognise the different sounds and to interpret them. This not only helps to encourage body awareness but helps the children to be aware of different sounds and rhythms and to be able to respond accordingly.

Teaching points

1. When using percussion so specifically it is wise to practise your rhythms very well beforehand so that you do not make mistakes during the lesson.

2. If working on the idea of movements which are close to the body contrasted with movements that go far away from the body, always emphasise the use of all the space around the body, and discourage always stretching into the same area.

LESSON FOUR

Main theme: Body awareness with emphasis on elbows and knees.

Sub-theme: Space awareness—movement on the spot and travelling using all the general space and emphasising change of direction.

Relationship: Dancing alone.

Introductory activity

Skipping all over the room or on the spot according to the sound on the tambourine (play the rhythm in a louder lively manner for travelling and in a more quiet, gentle manner for movement on the spot).

Movement training

1. Can you dance around the room with only one foot

touching the ground? Work at changing direction and going other ways than forwards. Can you make a pattern in the air with the other leg as you are travelling around?

2. Show me how the feet can dance around the room in lots of different ways (*e.g.* skip, jump, gallop, walk, etc.).

3. Running all over the room with tiny quiet steps. When the tambourine stops can you choose a shape to stop in?

4. As above, but this time when you stop can you make a shape in which your elbows and knees are important?

5. Can you make your elbows do a dance all around your body while your feet are still on the spot? What patterns can they make in the air?

6. Rub the elbows together and bounce them gently against each other.

7. Can your elbows reach right down and touch your knees?

Climax

Using the same phrasing and general pattern as in Lesson Two, work on skipping around the room this time concentrating on getting the knees high. Working on the spot, can the elbows do a skippy dance all around the body? Can you do a skipping dance all around the room making your knees and elbows very important? Use again the piece of music called *Boy and girl dance*. The children will know this well enough to begin to distinguish the different sections in the music and to know when to travel with feet and knees important; when to make the elbows dance on their own on the spot; and when to make all three dance around the room together.

Teaching points

1. When the children are moving on one foot only, make sure that you remind them to change at some time and work on the other foot or they will stay on the same foot all the time. In an activity of this sort it is not advisable to let it continue for any length of time as it is obviously more tiring than work on two feet.

2. In any running activity encourage the children to move on their toes.

3. Whenever the children make shapes stress the importance of the head being a part of the shape. So often the head is left out and they need constant reminders. Ask questions like: "What part is your head playing in the shape you have made?" "Is it looking up to the ceiling or down to the floor, or is it looking at the part of you that you are trying to make important in your shape?"

LESSON FIVE

Main theme: Body awareness with emphasis on elbows and knees.
Sub-theme: Space awareness—movement on the spot and travelling using all the general space.
Relationship: Dancing alone.

Introductory activity

Little quiet dotty jumps all over the room making patterns on the floor. (Again discourage travelling around the room in a circle and encourage continuous change of direction.)

Movement training

1. Walking around the room remembering all the different parts of the feet you can walk on. Which other ways can you walk besides going forwards all the time?

2. Walk with great big steps that reach out a long way as if you were trying to step right over large puddles. Can you put your feet down very carefully at the other side of the puddle so that you do not get splashed?

3. Contrast with 2 above. Can you walk with little tiny creeping steps as if you were trying to get past someone without waking them up?

4. Can you do a walking dance where you make the knees very important? Show me how you can do this marching dance in lots of different directions.

5. Can your elbows do a bouncy marching dance all around your body while you keep your feet still?

6. Can we make our feet and knees do a marching dance all over the room and see if our elbows can move in a bouncy marching way at the same time?

Climax

To a short piece of music called *Lively* with a distinct marching rhythm work at a little marching dance getting the knees high and moving with bouncy elbows at the same time. The space aspect of this climax is important, so encourage again the use of all the different directions including the idea of travelling with turning.

Teaching points

1. When working on the marching activity try to discourage the children from banging their feet into the ground. Instead put the emphasis on lifting their knees as high as they can.

2. When working on moving with elbows and feet together suggest that the elbows lead the rest of the body in changing direction, *e.g.* when the elbows are dancing in front of the body the feet travel forwards; when the elbows are dancing behind the body the feet travel backwards, and so on.

3. If using percussion to accompany the marching activity make sure that you play your rhythms at the same speed as it occurs in the music. The children then get used to the speed and are not confused when the music is introduced. This applies to any music which has a clearly defined rhythm.

LESSON SIX

Main theme: Body awareness—emphasis on knees, elbows and feet.
Sub-themes: Space awareness—travelling in different ways using the general space.
Awareness of weight and time—movements that are slow and light contrasted with movements that are sharp and sudden.
Relationship: Dancing alone.

Introductory activity

Running and jumping into all the spaces getting your knees up very high.

Movement training

1. Galloping around the room and on the spot lifting the the knees up as high as you can.

2. On the spot—can you make curving, circling patterns with one of your elbows all around your body? This makes the body stretch and bend, twist and turn and open and close.

3. Working with both elbows. Can they come slowly together until they touch each other and then shoot apart? Repeat several times and try to get the elbows to shoot apart in different directions each time.

4. Can your elbows reach slowly down to touch your knees and then shoot the body up into the air again?

5. Work again at marching all over the room in different directions making the elbows and knees work very hard.

6. Let your feet dance around the room in lots of different ways (reminder of skipping, jumping, etc.).

Climax

As well as using a piece of music we now have the added stimulus of a small story idea. The story divides into three parts as eventually does the dance. Each part of the dance is done to a different short piece of music.

THE TOY SOLDIERS

1. A little boy once had a box of beautiful toy soldiers given to him for his birthday. He plays with them for quite a long time until one day he is given something more exciting to play with. He collects them up, puts them in a box, and puts the box away in the toy cupboard. There they stay for many years until the little boy has grown up and gone away. Then one day another little boy comes to visit the house and is told he can choose something to play with out of the toy cupboard (this is the point in the story at which the dance starts). When he opens the door out falls the box of toy soldiers. They are not beautiful and shiny and new any more but old and dull with the paint flaking off them. The little boy tries to stand them up but at first they keep

falling over. Eventually, however, he does manage to stand them up, and

2. They are so pleased that they march around the room and then, stopping, they bow to the little boy to thank him and then off they go marching again. In fact, they are so pleased at being able to move again that

3. They forget all about marching and enjoy using their feet to dance all over the room. However, they are too old to keep dancing for long and eventually they fall back to the floor again. The little boy gathers them up and puts them back in the box and away they go in the toy cupboard again.

The dance

Section 1. Children begin in a small shape on the floor. With jerky movements of different body parts they begin to grow. The first two times they flop back to the floor, but the third time they stay on their feet (at this stage the movement training for this section has not been covered).

Music: *Intent*, Listen and Move No. 3 (Green Label).

Section 2. The children begin their marching dance using elbows, knees and feet. They bow to the little boy by making their elbows come slowly down to meet their knees and then bouncing them up high again. Then they march again.

Music: *Lively*, Listen and Move No. 3 (Green Label).

Section 3. The children enjoy dancing with their feet in lots of different ways until gradually they get slower and begin to curl up one by one back to their small shape on the floor.

Music: *Nimble*, Listen and Move No. 3 (Green Label).

At this stage in Lesson Six we would tell the children the story, and to finish with would use the piece of music called *Nimble* and the children would enjoy moving to it making their feet dance in lots of different ways.

Teaching points

1. Children find the galloping activity rather difficult. It will help them to gain height if they are encouraged to use their arms as well in the activity.

2. When working on the idea of elbows that meet and part try to help the children in using every part of the space around their bodies, *i.e.* one elbow high and one low, one in front and one behind, etc.

LESSON SEVEN

Main theme: Body awareness—use of individual body parts and whole body movement.

Sub-themes: Space awareness—going and stopping, movement on the spot, rising and sinking.

Awareness of weight and time—contrast between jerky, spiky movements and smooth, gentle movements.

Relationship: Dancing alone.

Introductory activity

Skipping all over the room making different parts of the foot important.

Movement training

1. Travelling with small, quiet running steps. Can you stop as if frozen when the tambourine stops? What sort of shape have you chosen to stop in?

2. Show me a spiky shape. Can you make every bit of you as pointed and jagged as it can be? Where are your head and eyes looking?

3. Travelling with little steps as in 1, but this time stopping in a spiky shape when the tambourine stops.

4. Show me how your fingers can do a spiky dance all around your body. Can other parts of your body move in a spiky way until last of all your feet join in and take you off around the room in a spiky, travelling dance?

5. Curl up small on the floor. Listen to the tambourine playing a very quiet tune and show me how you can grow in a smooth, gentle way until you are tall.

6. Curl up small again, but this time show me how you can grow in a jerky, spiky way with perhaps your elbows or fingers leading the way.

7. Still growing in a spiky way show me how you can grow

a little way and stop in a spiky shape, a little more and stop in a spiky shape, and then right up tall until your spiky shape collapses and you flop back to the floor and have to start growing all over again. Repeat this movement pattern again completely and then again until you have reached your tall shape and this time instead of falling back to the floor get your elbows, feet and knees ready for your marching dance.

Climax

Play the music called *Intent* and let the children listen and see if they can recognise the phrases for growing and pausing and the final phrase for flopping back to the floor. Try this through to the music at least twice. The children have now completed all three sections of the dance and are ready in the next lesson to try and put the whole story together.

Teaching points

1. When working on body shape encourage the children to make sure that elbows, knees, shoulders, fingers, heads, etc. are all part of the shape.

2. In Movement training 3 repeat the going and stopping phrase several times and suggest that the children choose a different spiky shape to stop in each time. Shapes might reach up to the ceiling, be close to the floor, twist in the centre, etc. Do not let them be content with the usual "middle" shapes.

3. Be careful that the children do not collapse heavily on the floor and hurt themselves. They might collapse bit by bit like a puppet when one string at a time is let go.

LESSON EIGHT

Main theme ⎫
Sub-theme ⎬ *See* Lesson Seven.
Relationship ⎭

Introductory activity

Let your feet dance all round the room in lots of different

ways travelling in different directions and going other ways besides forwards.

Movement training

The teacher must use the movement training section of this lesson to revise movements done in previous lessons, and in particular to give additional help in any part of the dance that is weaker than the rest.

Climax

With the children sitting tell again the story of the soldiers and then let them listen to the three pieces of music in the right order. With you telling the story as they move they are now able to put the three little dances together and dance the story of the "Toy Soldiers." Let them dance it at least twice so that having put it all together they can really enjoy it the second time with the security of knowing what to do next.

8
SERIES OF LESSONS FOR TOP INFANTS OR LOWER JUNIORS, BASED ON A VARIETY OF STIMULI

CIRCUS DANCE (four lessons)

Stimulus: The idea of a circus and various characters within it. It is hoped that the children will have worked previously on the theme "Body Awareness' with emphasis on hands and feet and elbows and knees, and two of the characters have been chosen to continue this work and two to introduce a new theme. The characters are—circus ponies, tight-rope walkers, jugglers and strong men.

Music: Ponies—*Quaint dance*, Listen and Move No. 5.
Tight-rope walker—*Quiet Mood No. 1*, Listen and Move No. 2.
Strong man—*Appalachian Spring*, Listen, Move and Dance No. 2 (H.M.V.).
Juggler—*Jolly little tune*, Listen and Move No. 2.

LESSON ONE

Main theme: Body awareness with emphasis on hands, feet and knees.

Sub-theme: Space awareness with emphasis on travelling and movements on the spot.

Relationship: Dancing alone.

Introductory activity

Running and jumping all over the room. Think about the different shapes that can be made in the air and emphasise landing lightly.

Movement training

1. Explore afresh all the different ways of using the feet to travel about the room. Think about changing direction and not always travelling forwards.

2. Move with little bouncy jumps all over the room, making a pattern on the floor as you go.

3. Walk about the room using all the space. Work at moving on different parts of the foot and sometimes varying the size, speed or level of the step.

4. Gallop all over the room. Think of the light, daintier gallop of the circus pony. Try to gallop in this way, lifting your knees up high. What patterns does a circus pony make? Can you make a pattern as you gallop?

5. Work a little on the hands.

(*a*) Shaking in all different directions.

(*b*) Rubbing one against the other. Feel each part rubbing against every other part.

(*c*) Hands which clap. Can you make different parts of the hands clap against each other?

(*d*) Can the hands make a galloping sound all around you on the floor?

Climax

With the children sitting, talk a little bit about the circus and the characters in the dance. Ask the children to describe for you what the characters are like and how they move. Play them the four short pieces of music and see if they can guess which piece fits which character. To finish the lesson let the children try the circus pony section to the music. Encourage change of direction and making the knees important.

LESSON TWO

Main theme:	Body awareness with emphasis on hands, knees and feet.
Sub-theme:	Space awareness with emphasis on travelling contrasted with movement on the spot using all the space around the body.
Relationship:	Dancing alone.

Introductory activity

Skipping all over the room using all the space. Listen to the sound on the tambourine and see if your skips can match the sound, sometimes skipping with large skips and sometimes with tiny ones.

Movement training

1. Running all over the room with light, quiet steps. Can you stop still whenever the tambourine stops?

2. Show how your feet can dance in lots of different ways as you travel around the room.

3. Listen to the tambourine playing a galloping rhythm. Sometimes it will play loudly and sometimes softly. See if you can match the different sounds with a galloping dance, sometimes about the room and sometimes on the spot. Can you think of any other ways a circus pony might move, *e.g.* trotting, pawing the ground, etc.

4. Work with hands:

(*a*) With hands close together, let them grow slowly apart until they are as far away from each other as possible, then bring them together again very quickly. Repeat several times, encouraging the children to let their hands grow apart in a different direction each time.

(*b*) Let your hands have a conversation with each other, moving near to each other, one following the other, etc. Watch your hands as they dance together.

5. Imagine there is a small rubber ball in front of you on the floor. Pick it up and feel the shape of it. Balance it on one hand and see if you can move it all around you without dropping it. Show how you can bounce this imaginary ball on the floor. Can you bounce it near to the floor, high into the air, right around you, as you walk, etc.

Climax

Listen to the music for the juggler. Show how many ways you can make the ball bounce as you dance to the music moving on the spot and travelling in different directions.

Main theme: Body awareness with emphasis on hands and feet and whole body movement.

Sub-themes: (*i*) Awareness of weight and time, light and slow movement contrasted with movements that are strong and slow.

           (*ii*) Space awareness—movement on the spot and travelling; changes of direction and pathway; change of level.

Relationship: Dancing alone.

Introductory activity

Running around the room with small steps, using quick movements of the shoulders and feet to avoid other children.

Movement training

1. Remind me of all the different ways you can walk about the room, remembering different pathways, different parts of the foot, different levels, ways other than forwards, big steps and little steps, etc.

2. Can you walk with very strong steps that try to push a hole in the floor, perhaps starting with the toes and lowering each part successively until the whole foot is pressed down into the floor?

3. Now as a contrast show how you can move with careful, slow, quiet steps about the room. Think of the tight-rope walker and show me how he would move. Choose a big space and imagine you have a tight-rope. How can you move along this tight-rope in a slow, careful way? Try to music.

4. Imagine again that you have a ball in your hands. Remind me of the different ways you can bounce this ball. Can you throw the ball from hand to hand, sometimes low, sometimes high, sometimes behind you, so that the whole body stretches, bends and twists. Experiment and see if you can juggle with any other parts of your body.

Climax

The children have now done a certain amount of work on three characters—the ponies, the tight-rope walkers and the jugglers. Play all three pieces of music to remind them of each. To finish with, let them try to dance each character with the music trying to bring out the contrasting movements of each.

Main theme: Awareness of weight and time with emphasis on movement that is strong and slow (all sorts of pushing, pressing, lifting and lowering movements).

Sub-themes: (*i*) Body awareness—emphasis on whole body movement.
               (*ii*) Space awareness—movements on the spot and travelling.

Relationship: Dancing alone.

Introductory activity

Begin the lesson with galloping, trotting, etc. to the appropriate music. Encourage the children to make a little pattern as they gallop, varying their direction and whether they travel or move on the spot, etc.

Movement training

1. Show me a strong shape. Is every part of you strong? (Choose a child who is making a good shape and see if the other children can tell you why it is good. Look for feet apart, knees bent, middles slightly contracted, head down as an extension of the general shape, clenched fists or strong, pressing palms).

2. When you have found a really strong shape, show how you can move around the room staying strong. Let your whole body help you as you press your feet into the ground. (Contrast this with light, quiet steps to give the children a release of tension. Perhaps accompany on the tambourine and make a rhythm contrasting strong, slow steps with light, slow ones.)

3. Keeping your strong shape, show me how you can lift up something heavy and put it down again and how you can pull and push it, using your whole body to help you. (Again,

look at some good shapes and see if the children can tell you why they are good.)

4. Listen to the "strong man" music and then show how you can move to it with strong, slow movements that travel and strong, slow movements on the spot.

Climax

Let the children work at both the "strong man" and the "tight-rope walker" to the music, trying to feel and bring out the contrast in effort involved in each activity.

We now have the basic movement pattern for the "Circus dance" and can develop it in any way. It may be necessary to spend longer on some aspects of the movement training that are less easy than others. How you develop this as a dance will depend on the ability and response of your children. With a class of young infants you may have each child dancing each character as the dance develops. An older, more experienced class are quite able to cope with group work which follows more closely the pattern of the circus. All the children might dance the circus pony, the activity leading them into three groups at the end of the music, each group representing one of the other three characters. The groups might dance one after the other, finishing the dance by repeating once again the movements of the circus pony.

THE MAGIC TOYSHOP (four lessons)

Stimulus: Short story idea. Every night when the clock strikes twelve all the toys in the toyshop begin to come alive. They spend the hours until daylight dancing and enjoying themselves. The rocking horse rocks right off his rockers and gallops about the toy shop. The jack-in-the-box springs right out of his box and enjoys bouncing all about the shop. The dancing doll winds herself up and dances gently, while the stringed puppet does his jerky dance. At the first sign of daylight the toys dance back to their places, and no-one ever knows that they have been alive.

Music: Rocking horse—*Gallop*, Listen and Move No. 5.
          Dancing doll—*Melodious*, Listen and Move No. 3.
          Puppet—*Mechanical doll*, Listen and Move No. 4.
          Jack-in-the-box—*Hop Scotch*, Listen, Move and
          Dance No. 1, Side 1 (H.M.V.).

LESSON ONE

Main theme: Space awareness with emphasis on changes of
               level, rising and sinking.
Sub-themes: (*i*) Body awareness—emphasis on growing in
               different ways. Activities of the feet.
               (*ii*) Awareness of weight and time, contrasting
               spikiness with smooth, light movement.
Relationship: Dancing alone.

Introductory activity

Running, making a pattern all over the floor and stopping
still when the tambourine stops.

Movement training

1. Can you make (*a*) a high shape—stretched towards the
ceiling; (*b*) a wide shape—spread and reaching outwards;
(*c*) a small shape—curled up and ball-like. When the
tambourine bangs see if you can change very quickly from
one shape to another.

2. Running again with small steps and each time the
tambourine stops choose one of these shapes to stop in.

3. Little tiny, high steps right up on your toes contrasted
with long, low steps down towards the floor. (The teacher
might play the tambourine to suggest a change from one to
the other.)

4. Let your feet take you on a dance all over the room,
going high, low and in and out with turning, twisting,
jumping, etc.

5. Show me a small shape on the floor. Can you grow very
smoothly and slowly until you are as big as you can be. Spin
all the way back to the floor again.

6. Can you use your hands to lead you as you grow? They

may make a gentle, curving pattern that turns you and lifts you higher and higher.

7. Listen to the tambourine playing a short, sharp sound. Can you grow in a jerky, spiky way with fingers, elbows and heads leading the way?

8. Can you grow very suddenly with one big jump as if you have exploded into the air? When you have grown can you go on a bouncy, jumping dance all over the room making a zig-zag pattern on the floor?

Climax

Tell the children about the magic toyshop Let them listen to the music for the "Jack-in-the-box." To finish let them make a small shape on the floor. When the music starts the children shoot right up out of their boxes and bounce all over the room. Encourage them to use their whole bodies to bounce high and low and in all different directions.

LESSON TWO

Main theme:	Body awareness with emphasis on hands and feet.
Sub-theme:	Space awareness—using the space all around the body contrasted with travelling in the general space.
Relationship:	Dancing alone.

Introductory activity

Running and jumping all about the room. Can you make wide, tall, small and twisted shapes in the air?

Movement training

1. Small bouncy jumps that take you all over the floor. Can you sometimes jump with feet close together and sometimes with feet apart?

2. Let your feet take you dancing in a curving, twisting pattern on the floor.

3. Think of the rocking horse and how he can gallop. Can you gallop about the room lifting your knees very high perhaps pretending sometimes to jump right over something?

4. Sitting. Shake your hands all about you in the space. Reach out into every corner.

5. Let your hands and fingers move very gently all around you in the space as if they were exploring and feeling their way.

6. Can your fingertips tap the floor lightly all around you?

7. Make a small shape on the floor. Can you grow with a rocking movement, swaying and rising higher and higher and quicker and quicker until your feet take you galloping off about the room?

Climax

Listen to the music for the rocking horse. Choose a shape near to the floor and rocking slowly at first get quicker and quicker until you gallop away to the music. Remember high knees, jumping, tossing heads, etc. The rocking horse is happy to be free.

LESSON THREE

Main theme: Awareness of weight and time. Smooth, curving movement contrasted with sharp, angular movement.

Sub-theme: Body awareness. Leading the movement with specific body parts.

Relationship: Dancing alone.

Introductory activity

Skipping in and out amongst each other with big, lively skips. Listen to the tambourine. When it plays quietly can you change to small, gentle skips?

Movement training

1. Walking with sharp, spiky steps that take you on an angular pathway on the floor.

2. Small, light running steps weaving in and out and making a curving, twisting pathway on the floor.

3. Sitting. Hold out your hands. Can you move them in a sharp, spiky way? Can they do a spiky dance all about you

in the air, sometimes coming very close to your body and sometimes dancing right away from it?

4. Show me how your hands can do a gentle dance about you, making a curving pattern in the air.

5. Make a small shape on the floor. Can your hands lead you in a gentle, curving way until you grow and grow and stop in a curved shape?

Climax

Listen to the music for the "Dancing doll." Can your hands lead you travelling and turning in a gentle, quiet dance all over the room?

LESSON FOUR

Main theme ⎫
Sub-theme ⎬ As Lesson Three.
Relationship ⎭

Introductory activity

Walking all over the room, making different parts of the feet important, *e.g.* heels which shoot up behind, etc.

Movement training

1. Careful, quiet steps touching the floor gently with the feet so as not to make a sound.

2. Skipping with jerky, spiky knees.

3. Sitting. Let your fingers and hands do a jerky, spiky dance around you. Can any other part of you join in with your hands and do a spiky dance as well? For instance, heads, shoulders, elbows.

4. Tuck up small on the floor. Choose one part of your body to lead you growing in a spiky way until you have made a big, spiky shape. Flop back to the floor again. Repeat several times as if you were a puppet and someone is jerking the strings to lift you up onto your feet.

Climax

Listen to the music for the "puppet." See if you can grow in a jerky way and then dance about the room with spiky steps and jerky movements of different body parts.

These four lessons are complete within themselves. The teachers of infants may wish to use the lessons in serial form unfolding the story week by week. In this way the children need not remember work done in previous lessons. Junior teachers may prefer to use the lessons as a build up, the climax being a further lesson or lessons when revision is made of the various aspects of movement training and all four sections of the dance are put together to create a whole.

WINTER DANCE (five lessons)
Stimulus: Poem.

Winter Fun

The snow kept falling through the night,
Crystal flakes of shimmering white
Came gently drifting, floating down
Upon the silent, sleeping town.

The children playing out next day,
Keeping warm and feeling gay,
Make footprint patterns in the snow,
And we can see just where they go,

As off into the woods they run,
Just watch and see how they have fun;
While snowballs hurtle through the air
And we all wish that we were there.

But someone else is watching, too—
It's old Jack Frost: what will he do?
He'll make them shiver—wait and see;
Poor frozen statues they will be.

And in a quick· dance off he goes,
Nipping at their feet and toes.
He's happy now he's found a way
To tease the children as they play.

But look! The sun comes out at last;
Our Jack Frost's merry game is past.
The warmth will melt him right away—
He'll have to play another day.

O how the time has quickly gone.
The children's games are nearly done.
The sun has almost left the sky
As happy voices call "Good-bye!"

Music: Snow falling—*Flute Sonata*, Listen, Move and Dance No. 2 (H.M.V.).
Footprint patterns—*Perky*, Listen and Move No. 3 (Green Label).
Snowball fight—*Intent*, Listen and Move No. 3 (Green Label).
Shivery—*Quivering Pipe*, Listen and Move No. 4 (Green Label).
Jack Frost—*Mechanical doll*, Listen and Move No. 4 (Green Label).
Children—*Nimble*, Listen and Move No. 3 (Green Label).

LESSON ONE

Main theme: Body awareness with emphasis on hands and feet.

Sub-themes: (*i*) Awareness of weight and time—light, delicate movements of different body parts.
(*ii*) Space awareness—changing levels; different pathways.

Relationship: Dancing alone.

Introductory activity

With feet close together can you make a little bouncy jumping dance all over the room? What sort of pattern are you making on the floor?

Movement training

1. Running very quickly in and out amongst each other. Can you stop very still when the tambourine stops?

2. Travelling with little tiny steps, on the toes. Can you travel in and out and round and round, sometimes dancing up to the ceiling and sometimes down to the floor?

Sitting

3. Shake your hands all about you in the space.
4. Clap your hands together. Can you find any other parts of your hands to bounce against each other?
5. Make a very loud noise on the floor with your hands.
6. Let your fingertips dance very lightly on the floor. Can they go on dancing lightly and weave a curving, gentle pattern all around you in the space?
7. Standing. Can your feet and fingers do a light, gentle dance together as you travel about the room?

Climax

Read the children the poem. Listen to the music for the "falling snow." Imagine the snow falling and being blown gently by the wind so that it lifts and falls and makes a pattern in the sky. With the music work again at light feet and fingers dancing and sinking silently to the floor when the music stops.

LESSON TWO

Main theme: Body awareness concentrating on jumping activities of the feet.
Sub-theme: Space awareness—changes of pathway and direction.
Relationship: Partner work.

Introductory activity

Running and jumping all over the room. Can you change your shape in the air each time you jump?

Movement training

1. Walking about the room changing direction. Imagine you are walking on crisp, white snow and making footprint patterns as you go. Sometimes big steps, sometimes little ones, sometimes retracing your steps, travelling backwards, forwards, sideways, round and round.

2. Can your feet dance all over the room in lots of different ways?

3. Can you do a jumping dance where your feet are sometimes close together and sometimes far apart?

4. Find a partner. With your partner, can you make up a little pattern of steps and jumps, thinking again about making a pattern in the snow? Are you going to make your pattern side by side or one behind the other, or will you travel towards each other and away? Are you both going to work together all the time or one and then the other? Think about change of direction, change of level, size of step and jump, etc.

Climax

Listen to the music for the footprint patterns. Can you work with your partner to the music, seeing if you can repeat your pattern several times?

LESSON THREE

Main theme: Body awareness with emphasis on feet and basic body shapes—wide, tall, small, twisted.
Sub-theme: Space awareness—going and stopping.
Relationship: Dancing alone.

Introductory activity

Running all over the room with very quick steps that take you weaving in and out of everyone else.

Movement training

1. Running and stopping. Imagine you are running and hiding behind differently shaped trees so that you stop in different shapes—wide, tall, small, twisted. Hold your shapes very still.

2. Sitting. Imagine again that the ground is covered with snow. Can you make patterns and shapes in it with different parts of your hands, e.g. sides, fingertips, knuckles, palms, backs, fists, etc.

3. Pick up a handful of snow. Can you make it into a

hard, round ball? Put it on the ground. Can you roll it and roll it until it becomes a giant ball?

4. You are in the woods with your friends and enjoy having a snowball fight. (In order that this doesn't develop into a "free for all" it is important that the teacher phrases the activity and accompanies it with voice or percussion.)

The music for this activity consists of four identical phrases, each broken up into smaller patterns which suggest three slower actions followed by a quick movement. This could be used in this way:

This phrase would repeat three times with the children choosing a different shape to stop in each time.

Climax

Let the children listen to the music for the "snowball fight" and try their little phrase of movement to it. Encourage the children to use their whole body in the throw.

LESSON FOUR

Main theme: Awareness of weight and time—sharp, spiky movements contrasted with light, shaking movements.

Sub-themes: (i) Space awareness—rising and sinking activities, movement on the spot and travelling.

(ii) Body awareness—making different parts of the body important.

Relationship: Dancing alone.

Introductory activity

Skipping all over the room. Can you make different parts of your feet important as you skip (heels which shoot up behind, etc.)?

Movement training

1. Walking with very sharp, spiky steps making an angular pathway on the floor.

2. Hide your hands away behind your back or tuck them in very close to your body. Listen for a loud sound on the tambourine. Can you shoot your hands away from you to make a spiky shape? (Repeat several times, encouraging the children to shoot their hands out in a different direction each time).

3. Make a small shape near the floor. When the tambourine bangs can you choose just one part of your body and let it shoot right away from you? It may be your head or a leg or arm (repeat several times).

4. Still in a small shape. Can you choose one part of your body to lead you growing in a spiky way?

5. Think about Jack Frost and how he freezes everything up when he does his sharp, icy dance. Can you move like this with spiky elbows, fingers, shoulders and heads freezing the tall things and sharp feet and knees freezing things near to the floor?

Climax

Listen to the "shivery" music. When the children have finished their snowball fight they begin to feel cold and start to shiver with different parts of their bodies. As they get colder and colder Jack Frost grows up from his small shape, and as the "Jack Frost" music begins he continues his icy dance about the room, turning the children into statues. Here the class could divide into two halves, one representing the children and one Jack Frost, with each dancing to the appropriate music. Allow time for the children to change over, giving each an opportunity to move to both pieces of music.

LESSON FIVE

Main theme } All aspects are brought together in this lesson.
Sub-themes }
Relationship: Dancing alone, partner work, class halved.

Introductory activity

With the last piece of music. Can your feet take you dancing all over the room to the music? Let your whole body be a part of this dance—fingers, elbows, heads, middles, knees, etc.

Movement training

In this lesson the teacher might revise some of the movement training done in previous lessons preparatory to putting the whole dance together at the end of the lesson.

Climax

Read the poem again to the children and remind them of the different parts of the dance. Try all through to the music.

Teachers of junior classes might wish to divide the children into groups in the last lesson so that they have less movement on which to concentrate. The dance divides naturally into three groupings—(a) the snow; (b) the children; (c) Jack Frost. Teachers of infant classes might prefer to use some of these ideas for isolated lessons on various aspects of winter, linking the work with topics in the classroom.

LATE FOR WORK

Stimulus: A poem.

Late for Work

> Tucked up warm and fast asleep,
> Wandering in the land of dreams.
> While the daylight, filtering through,
> Says good-bye to moonlight beams.
>
> Suddenly, a harsh, loud ring.
> What a noise! It's that alarm.
> Pull the bedclothes overhead—
> A minute more will do no harm.
>
> Stretch and turn and slowly lift
> One leg, two legs, out of bed.
> It's time to rise and face the day;
> Stir yourself, you sleepy-head.

Goodness me! Is that the time?
You'll have to rush to catch the train.
Wash yourself and get dressed quick,
Or you'll be late for work again.

There's no time for breakfast now—
Through the door and close the gate,
To the station just in time, to hear
Them say, "Your train is late!"

Sit a moment, catch your breath;
Watch the signals rise and drop.
Metal pointers, sharp and sudden,
Tell you that your train will stop.

Now, at last, the train is coming.
Hear the whistle! Clear the way!
Look at all the people rushing—
You won't find a seat do-day.

As the engine gathers speed,
Fields and hedgerows all rush by.
Horses grazing, rather frightened,
Gallop off, manes tossing high.

Why not walk down to the buffet—
Have a morning cup of tea.
Rattling train makes footsteps falter;
Rolls you like the waves at sea.

Here's your station! There's no time now—
Morning tea will have to wait.
You must make a resolution—
"To-morrow you will not be late!"

Suggested Music: *Waking—Scenes d'enfant*. Listen, Move and Dance No. 2 (H.M.V.).
Getting ready—No. 6 for Children. Listen, Move and Dance No. 1 (H.M.V.).
Signals—No. 29 For Children. Listen, Move and Dance No. 1 (H.M.V.).
Train—No. 4 Electronic Sound Pictures.

Listen, Move and Dance No. 4 (H.M.V. L.P.).
Horses—Gallop. Listen & Move No. 5 (Green Label).
Going to the buffet—Syncopated Tune. Listen and Move No. 5 (Green Label).

The poem suggests a number of different movement ideas and the teacher might wish to select just a few of these to interpret in movement. I have not included a series of lesson plans for this dance, but below is a list of movement training suitable for each section:—

Waking

The movement should be sustained and will include work on rising and sinking in different ways, gesture and changing body shapes. The children will begin in attitudes of sleep, low to the floor.

Getting ready

This movement is more mimetic, *e.g.* washing, cleaning teeth, getting dressed, running downstairs, putting on hat and coat, running to the station and stopping to cross the roads. This is a direct contrast with the sustained movement of the "waking".

Signals

Sharp, angular movements into space with different parts of the body, *e.g.* elbow joint, shoulders, heads, knees, wrists. Whole body movements up and down or forward and back suggesting the rise and fall of the signals.

Train

This music could be used just as a sound effect to link two parts of the dance. The teacher could spend time on acceleration and deceleration in movement to suggest the arrival and departure of the train.

Horses

A simple galloping activity accenting the knees and working on pathway on the floor.

Walking to the buffet

Walking at different speeds with sudden changes from one to the other. Changes of direction and level.

OTHER THEMES SUITABLE FOR THIS AGE GROUP

1. Journey into space—Take off, star patterns, touch down, moon walk, strange creatures, lift off.

2. Under the sea—Rock shapes, darting fish, seaweed patterns, sea monsters.

3. On the beach—Children playing, Punch & Judy, boats, storm at sea.

4. Noah's Ark—The rain, the big strong animals, the small light animals.

5. The seasons—Winter weather; spring beginning—plants, etc; summer sun and happiness; autumn—falling leaves, etc.

6. The street—Playing hopscotch, throwing and catching a ball, looking in shop windows, etc.

7. A trip to the park—Playing on the grass, on the swing, hide and seek, etc.

9

SERIES OF LESSONS FOR UPPER JUNIORS, BASED ON A VARIETY OF STIMULI

MACHINE DANCE (four lessons)

Stimulus:	A dance based on the idea of two different types of machinery—jerky and piston-like contrasted with curved and wheel-like.
Music:	*Syncopated Clock*, by Leroy Anderson.

LESSON ONE

Main theme:	Awareness of weight and time—emphasis on sharp, jerky movements contrasted with curving, smooth movements.
Sub-themes:	(*i*) Space awareness—contrast between flexible movements that use all the space and direct movements that travel in an angular pathway. Movements on the spot and travelling.
	(*ii*) Body awareness—changing body shapes. Emphasis on different body parts.
Relationship:	Dancing alone.

Introductory activity

Skipping all over the room, sometimes with big skips that use a lot of space and sometimes with little skips using only a small space. Work at change of direction.

Movement training

1. Stepping all over the room. Think of other ways to travel besides forwards.

2. Can you explore and find different parts of your feet to walk on?

3. Listen to the **tambourine**. See if you can decide when it

78

is suggesting long, lingering steps and when it is suggesting sharp, spiky ones. Can you match the sound on the tambourine? Now see if you can choose which one you are going to do first and change from one to the other without the tambourine helping you.

4. Can your hands and arms do a jerky, spiky dance in the space all around you? (Remember that wrists, elbows and shoulders are the joints which need to move to achieve real jerkiness).

5. Can your knees and feet take you travelling all over the room in a jerky dance? (Different parts of the feet can shoot out into space in different directions).

6. Think of the curving letters of the alphabet and curved numerals. Can you choose some and draw them in the air with your finger? Now use your whole arm and make them bigger. Try drawing them so big that your whole body must bend and stretch and twist to help you.

Climax

Let the children listen to the music first and see if they can pick out the two contrasting qualities. Discuss with them the different types of machinery. To finish the lesson let the children move to the jerky A section of the music and experiment with their own ideas of the jerky movements of machinery.

LESSON TWO

Main theme ⎫
Sub-themes ⎬ As Lesson One.
Relationship ⎭

Introductory activity

Running and jumping all over the room. Can you make a different shape in the air each time you jump?

Movement training

1. Show me how you can make a curved shape. Make sure that every part of you is smooth and rounded and no sharp corners are left sticking out (encourage shapes in different levels).

2. Can you change and choose a new curved shape? Listen to the tambourine and see if you can change in a smooth, gentle way (repeat several times).

3. This time show me how you can make a jagged, angular shape. Think of elbows, fingers, head, knees, feet, etc.

4. Can you change in a sharp, sudden way to make a new angular shape?

5. Still moving in a sharp, jerky way can you begin to create a moving machine? It might go up and down as well as along, forwards, backwards, sideways or around.

6. Now think of a machine made of wheels. Can you move in a curving, circling way all over the room using lots of space, turning and travelling low and high? (This activity could include cartwheels, spinning on the floor, etc.).

Climax

The music has the form A–A–B–A–C–A–A. Let the children begin to work more specifically on the first A–A–B sections. On the first A the machine begins to work in a jerky way but only on the spot. On the second A the machine (still jerky) begins to move and travel. On B the machine changes and becomes wheel-like and curving. All the movement material has been covered in the movement training, but the children will now be selecting and creating their own individual machines.

LESSON THREE

Main theme ⎫
Sub-themes ⎬ As Lesson One.
Relationship: Partner work.

Introductory activity

Travelling and turning using different directions and learning to make curving, twisting pathways on the floor.

Movement training

1. With feet together make a bouncy, jumping dance over the room. Can you create a zig-zag, angular pattern on the floor?

2. Make a small shape near the floor. Can you grow in a

sharp, jerky way and stop in an angular shape? Repeat several times, arriving in a different angular shape each time. Use the tambourine to phrase the growing.

3. With music—revise sections A–A–B worked at in the last lesson. Encourage the children to select little patterns of movement that they like doing and try to repeat them.

Climax

We move on now to the third A section of the music. Let the children take a partner and begin to experiment with the idea of creating a jerky, partner machine. Remember that starting position is important. Are they going to start close together, far apart, side by side, back to back, facing, on the same level, one high and one low? Are they both identical parts of the machine moving together and doing the same, or are they two completely different parts who perhaps move one after the other? Give the children opportunity to work both with and without the music.

LESSON FOUR

Main theme ⎫ As Lesson One.
Sub-themes ⎭
Relationship: Partner and group work.

Introductory activity

Skipping all over the room using all the space. Can you stop in an angular shape when the tambourine stops?

Movement training

1. Running in and out of everyone else making a curving, twisting, pathway on the floor.

2. Stepping with jerky, spiky steps making an angular pathway on the floor.

3. With partners, work at duo and give the children plenty of time to establish a small pattern of movement they can remember and repeat.

4. With music put dance together up to the end of partner section (A–A–B–A).

Climax

Listen to the C section of the music. This is a complete contrast to sections A and B. Put the children into three or four large groups and let them begin to work on the idea of a group machine. This can be either jerky or wheel-like or, if the children choose, a mixture of both. As in partner work, stress the importance of starting position and formation—circle, lines, irregular, etc. Again give the children opportunity to work both with and without the music.

These four lessons form the basis for the Machine Dance. It is up to the teacher and the children how it develops. The lessons have covered the sections A–A–B–A–C. In the remaining two A sections the children may revert to working individually. The music has a short coda which suggests the breakdown of the machinery. Probably this dance will take five to six lessons depending upon the needs of the children.

PRIMITIVE HUNT DANCE (3 lessons)

This dance is for the 9+ to 10+ age group in the junior school and would probably take several lessons as each section was built up.

Stimulus:	Dramatic idea of a primitive tribe where the women work in the village while the men go out to hunt for food.
Music:	*Ritual Dance* from Listen and Move No. 4 (Green Label), played twice.
Main theme:	Awareness of weight and time—emphasis on the changes of effort involved in a variety of occupational rhythms.
Sub themes:	(*i*) Body awareness—emphasis on different body parts.
	(*ii*) Space awareness—changes of level, movement on the spot, travelling in different pathways.
Relationship:	Duos and trios in the village. A small group of hunters. All join in one large group at the end of the dance.

Introductory activity

Some form of travelling activity, perhaps skipping, running and jumping, etc. Think about the pathway you are taking as you move about the room. Is it curved, twisted or angular?

Movement training

1. Work on travelling on the feet in different ways encouraging changes of direction and level and travelling in directions other than forwards.

2. Stepping all over the room without percussion accompaniment. Can you make your step pattern interesting by varying the size, speed, direction, part of foot, level, etc.

3. Stepping in time to the tambourine playing a $\frac{4}{4}$ rhythm. Can the children respond to the accented first beat either with an explosive jump pushing away from the floor or with a downward thrusting movement into the floor. We are beginning to build up a small rhythmic pattern that can be repeated over and over again.

4. Leave the children free to accent 1 in any way that they like and to find a way of travelling on 2, 3 and 4. Separate the class into two halves, one to work, the other to observe. This gives the workers more room and the observers a chance to see the patterns others have created (change over).

Observation points

(a) Are the children really accenting the first beat and making it different from the rest of the phrase?

(b) Are they repeating their little rhythm each time and how are they travelling?

(c) Is every part of their body involved in the activity?

5. Introduce one or two working activities that have a clearly defined rhythmic pattern, *e.g.* chopping down a tree can be tried by all the children, first in their own time and then put into a rhythmic phrase by the teacher with percussion accompaniment. Perhaps a small chop, a bigger chop, a great big chop, and rest. These words have their own

pattern as you say them. Work at holding the chopping implement, stance, parts of the body used, etc.

6. Choose a compensatory activity like throwing grain onto the soil from a basket. This is a travelling activity with a 1–2–3 rhythm of a gathering and scattering nature, and has a peaceful quality as opposed to the stronger static activity of chopping.

Climax

Play the music and talk about primitive times with the children. The music has the form A–B–A. Let the children work to Part B of the music and experiment with their primitive $\frac{4}{4}$ rhythms from earlier in the lesson.

LESSON TWO

Introductory activity

Running and jumping, trying to achieve different shapes in the air in the jump.

Movement training

1. Work again at primitive travelling rhythms from last lesson. Encourage the children to select and choose a small pattern of movement that they can repeat.

2. Think about the different working actions that might go on in the village, *i.e.* washing, fetching and carrying water, pounding grain, building, etc. Let each child choose a working action and try to phrase it into a small rhythmic pattern.

Climax

Divide the children into groups of two or three, each group choosing an activity which needs the participation of more than one person. Work on the rhythm of the activity. Stress the importance of watching the others. Children will need help from the teacher in deciding the right amount of effort to be put into each activity. Try the various working actions to the music—A section.

Introductory activity

In your own time revise your travelling primitive rhythm
What sort of pattern are you making on the floor?

Movement training

This will depend at this stage on the teacher's observations of
the children and what help she thinks they will need.

Climax

Try the whole dance together to the music. The music is
played twice, so the form will be A–B–A, A–B–A. Children are
divided into two groups. One group represents the hunters and
the others (divided into twos and threes) represent the women
working in the village.

On A(1) the hunters hold their positions at one end of the
room, while the women begin their working actions. On B(1)
the women continue working while the hunters travel around
the room with their primitive rhythms. They see the kill,
encircle it, and spear it. On A(2) the men hold their positions
over the kill and the women continue working, perhaps with a
development of their original motif. On A(3) the men lift their
kill and begin to carry it back to the centre of the village. As
they do so each group of women they pass stops working to
watch. On arriving in the centre of the village they put down
the kill and call the women to come and see. On B(2) the men
are still in a small circle around the kill, while the women
begin group by group to leave their work and form a larger
circle around the men to view the kill. On A(4) the whole
group do a dance of thanksgiving around the kill ending in a
triumphant position.

The teacher will see that these lessons form the bare bones of
the dance, leaving much room for the children's own ideas and
interpretations. It is obviously going to take more than three
lessons as both groups will need time to work on their own
sections. The children may wish to work out a set pattern for the
dance of triumph at the end.

MODELLING DANCE (five lessons)

Stimulus—a short story. A modeller has in his workshop a very large piece of stone, wood or clay and he sets out to make the most beautiful statue he has ever made. He chisels and presses and moulds it until it is made. Having admired his work he is so pleased with himself that he starts to dance around it. In fact, he has made the statue so well that to his amazement it begins to come alive. At first the modeller is very frightened, but when he gets over his shock he is really rather pleased. After all, he has such a lot of work to do and now at last he has someone to help him. So he sets about to teach the statue how to chisel and how to mould. The statue, however, does not want to be a servant, and taking the chisel he knocks his master out. Very pleased to be free, he dances around the master. In our dance, of course, we have lots of modellers and lots of statues, and now all the statues join together and push the masters into a heap in the middle of the room. Making a circle around them, they pretend to chisel and mould them into shape and then proceed to have a gay dance all around them. They are so busy enjoying themselves that they do not notice when the modellers begin to come back to life. When they do, they are very frightened because they know what is going to happen to them. Each modeller comes back to his statue in a very menacing way and, picking up his chisel, breaks his beautiful statue into little pieces.

Music: *Une petite cantata*, played by Paul Mauriat and his
orchestra.

LESSON ONE

Main theme: Body awareness with emphasis on using the hands and feet in different ways. Body shapes.

Sub-themes: (*i*) Awareness of weight and time—short, sharp, jerky movement contrasted with a stronger pressing activity.

(*ii*) Space awareness—exploring the areas of space around the body.

Relationship: Dancing alone.

Introductory activity

Running and jumping all over the room. What shapes can you make when you are in the air?

Movement training

1. Stepping using all the space in the room and concentrating on change of direction.

2. Stepping with quick, spiky steps making different parts of the feet important.

3. Stepping with strong steps that press downwards into the ground (this requires use of the whole body and is not a noisy, stamping activity).

4. Imagine you are in a small room with no windows or doors. Show me how you can use your hands to push very strongly at the walls, ceiling and floor.

5. Imagine that you have a hammer and chisel in your hands. How could you chisel a hole in those walls with short, sharp movements?

6. Using the space around you, make a little rhythmic pattern of chiselling and pressing ..../......../———— ——/—— ——/. Pretend you are creating a statue.

Climax

Tell the children the modeller's story and play them the music. The music has the form A–A–B–A–B–A–coda. A consists of four phrases. The first two of these have a light staccato quality which suggest chiselling or a short, sharp movement; the latter two phrases are stronger without the staccato and suggest a pressing movement, hence the phrasing

......../......../—— ——/—— ——//

chiselling chiselling press press press press
Having listened to the music, let the children experiment with this pattern in the space around them to the first two A sections of the music.

LESSON TWO

Main theme: Body awareness—emphasis on the feet and

leading the movement with specific parts of the body.

Sub-themes: As Lesson One.
Relationship: Partner work.

Introductory activity

Skipping all around the room and on the spot according to the sound on the tambourine. Can you skip in all different directions and high and low, twisting, weaving, and turning in and out of everyone else as you go?

Movement training

1. Can your feet dance in lots of different ways around the room, *e.g.* jumping, skipping, galloping, etc.

2. On the spot. Make a strong shape—strong fist, strong feet, etc.

3. Listen to the tambourine. Can you dance with your feet all around the room and when the tambourine stops choose a strong shape to stop in?

4. Still being strong, show me how you can press and push into the space all around you as if you were trying to move a heavy object. Which parts of your body can you push with?

5. Show me your elbows. Make them very pointed. Can they do a jerky, spiky dance all around you in the space, making your body stretch and bend and twist?

6. Remember the little pattern of chiselling and pressing from last lesson. Instead of holding a hammer and chisel, see if you can do short, sharp, chiselling movements with different parts of your body (use an accompaniment on the tambourine but try to keep the phrases the same length as in the music).

Climax

Find a partner. Decide which of you is going to dance the modeller and which the statue. The modeller is going to create a statue out of his partner, but he has to be very clever because he must do it without actually touching his partner. We work here on the idea of action and re-action, *e.g.* the modeller might choose to make an arm first, and as he does his short, sharp chiselling movement towards his partner's arm it will respond and grow in a jerky way. If he is kneeling and chiselling from underneath the arm, it will jerk upwards. If he is behind his partner, the arm will jerk forwards, etc. Remember the phrasing in A—two phrases of chiselling and two phrases of pressing; then A is repeated. To help the children you might suggest they make one arm first, then the other, and then perhaps press the head into shape. On the second A they might chisel one leg, then the other, and then lastly press the middle into shape. Let the children work first to your percussion accompaniment, and then try this small partner dance to the first two A sections of the music. They will need to listen to the music several times and learn to distinguish the different phrases.

LESSON THREE

Themes: As Lesson One.
Relationship: Continuing partner work.

Introductory activity

Skipping all over the room. Can you lift your knees very high as you travel?

Movement training

1. Show me your elbows. Can they make circling patterns around you in the space? (Remember the space above the body, below, behind, to the side, etc.).

2. Can your elbows lead you travelling all over the room, sometimes making you jump up to the ceiling, sometimes taking you near to the floor, sometimes turning you, etc.?

3. Running all over the room with very small steps. When the tambourine stops can you choose a statue shape to stop in? How can you make this statue come alive? Is it going to stretch, slowly, or will it jerk to wake itself up? Maybe it comes alive in a burst. (Repeat pattern of running, pausing and waking several times and encourage the children to find a different way of waking each time.)

4. With partners. Go over Section A–A from last week and give help to individual couples if needed.

Climax

Let the children work again on Section A–A to the music. Sit and listen to music B. This is where the modeller dances all around the statue he has made and then stops as the statue begins to wake. Remind the children of the parts of the movement training relevant to this.

1. Letting the elbows lead the modeller in a travelling, jumping, turning dance all around his statue.

2. How is the statue going to come alive and how does the modeller react?

Let the children try Section B on its own with the music. We are now able to put A–A–B together as the climax to our lesson, and our story in movement is beginning to take shape.

LESSON FOUR

Themes: As previous lessons.
Relationship: Partner work—shadowing or mirroring.

Introductory activity

Let your elbows lead you in a dance all over the room using all the space, dancing sometimes high, sometimes low.

Movement training

1. At this stage the earlier part of the movement training will depend upon the teacher's observation of her class. A certain amount of help and revision will be needed on work from previous weeks, and the children will need to refresh their memories.

2. In twos. We left the dance at the point where the statue had come alive. In the story the modeller now begins to teach the statue how to chisel and press, and we have reached another A in the music. The children will by now know the phrasing and rhythm of the A tune and should be able to make up little partner dances using the two movements.

Teaching points

1. What is your starting position going to be? Are you facing each other or side by side?

2. Which part of the body is the modeller going to teach his partner to chisel with? It should be clear from the starting position.

3. There are two phrases of chiselling. Is the statue going to mirror his partner or is the modeller going to chisel first and then be still while his partner copies him?

4. Can the modeller teach his partner to chisel and press in different places in space and not just in front of his nose? If so, are they starting high, low, or out to one side, etc.?

The teacher should accompany this partner work on the tambourine but must make sure that the phrases are the same length as those in the music. This gives the children a chance to build up their little dance bit by bit until they have made a pattern that they like and can remember. Individual help will be needed and the teacher should move around the hall giving any help she thinks necessary.

Climax

At the end of the lesson let the children put their little dance to the music. Let them try several times to give them a chance to sort out anything that went wrong. To finish the lesson work from the beginning of the dance to this point. A–A–B–A.

LESSON FIVE

Themes: As previous lessons.
Relationship: Partner leading into a group dance.

Introductory activity

1. Walking all over the room using all the space.

2. Show me how you can do very strong steps that push down into the floor. Use your whole body to help you be strong.

3. Can you walk with little spiky steps that make a pointed pattern on the floor?

4. Listen to the tambourine. Can you tell when it is saying strong and slow or quick and spiky? See if your steps can match the tambourine.

Movement training

1. Show me a very strong shape with flat palms ready to make a pressing movement. Imagine you are pushing something very heavy in front of you (with tambourine play a little rhythm for pushing and resting).

2. Go with your partner and see if you can remember your little partner dance from last lesson. Practise it several times.

Climax

We are now ready to add the rest of our story. When the modeller has taught the statue how to chisel and press, the statue very ungratefully knocks him out. Stress the importance of "not touching your partner." This is again action and re-action. Perhaps some modellers can fall to the ground while others stay on their feet but let their top halves collapse rather like a puppet when the strings go loose. The statue now dances all around the modeller to the second B section of the music and ends on the outside of the room in a strong shape with palms ready to push towards the modeller, who responds by moving towards the middle of the room (how will he move?). We now have all the modellers making a group shape in the middle of the room and all the statues in a circle on the outside. When the fourth A theme returns the statues all repeat the chiselling, pressing motif towards the group in the centre as if they were trying to create a large statue. On B(3) the statues dance in and out towards the group with elbows leading, but while they are dancing the modellers begin to awake and to come back towards their statues. The statues cower, and on the little coda at the end of the music the modellers chisel them back into shapelessness.

Synopsis of music, movement and story

Music:	A(1)	Modellers creating statues with short, sharp, chiselling movements and stronger, pressing movements.
	A(2)	
	B(1)	Modellers admiring statues, dancing around them and showing fear as their statues come alive (elbows lead in jumping, turning, travelling).

A(3)   Partner dance. Modeller teaches statue how to chisel and press, but at the end the statue knocks the modeller out.

B(2)   Statue dances around the fallen modeller (elbows lead in jumping, turning, travelling). Statue ends on outside and pushes modeller towards centre of room.

A(4)   Statues repeat little chisel and press pattern towards group in the centre of the room.

B(3)   Statues dance in towards centre group and out again (elbows lead in travelling, turning, jumping). Modellers awake and come back to statues in a menacing manner.

Coda.   Modellers chisel statues back into shapelessness.

FIREWORK DANCE

Stimulus: A dance based on the actions of four different fireworks. These fireworks have been chosen for their contrasting effort qualities and varied use of space.

(i) Rip-rap (jumping cracker). This firework moves in a sharp, jerky way, usually on an angular or zig-zag pathway.

(ii) Roman candle. This firework rises from the ground in a series of movements, falling away in a variety of patterns on the spot.

(iii) Catherine wheel. This firework has a spinning, turning action with suggestions of spiky, sparking patterns.

(iv) Rocket. This firework shoots out into space, falling away in a series of stars.

If the teacher wishes to begin the dance with a common activity she can take the idea of the movements of a bonfire. The children may begin in a large group shape in the centre of a room representing the shape of a bonfire. To a short, sharp accompaniment by the teacher, those children on the outer edge of the group will begin to move with sudden, sharp, flickery movements perhaps beginning in one body part only. As other body parts join in the movement gradually passes through the rest of the group and the bonfire is truly alight. As the flames begin to rise the movement gets stronger until sparks begin to fly from the bonfire and the children move away from the centre of the room with jumping, darting, turning movements to meet in four groups, each group ready to represent one of the four fireworks.

Main themes: (*i*) Space awareness—different forms of travelling, changes of level, exploration of space words, *e.g.* spinning, shooting, darting, billowing, etc., all of which suggest a different use of space.

(*ii*) Awareness of weight and time—contrasting spikiness with smooth movement.

Sub-theme: Body awareness—emphasis on different body parts, whole body movement, activities on the feet.

Relationship: Large group leading to smaller groups.

Accompaniment: Percussion and vocal sounds made initially by the teacher and then by the children themselves in their group work.

As so much of the finished product is going to depend on the ideas of the children themselves in their groups I am just going to suggest ideas for movement training rather than set out specific lesson plans. Movement training should include:

1. All sorts of spinning, turning, wheel-like activities. These could include turning of the whole body, gestures of different body parts to suggest the shape of a wheel, spinning movements on the floor on different body parts, cartwheels, etc. The children should be encouraged to spin in different levels and to travel from one level to another.

2. Travelling activities on the feet including quick little jumps and sharp, spiky movements of the feet that make an angular, zig-zag pattern on the floor.

3. Rising and sinking, opening and closing in a variety of different ways using different body parts in gesture to create patterns in space.

4. Spiky movements of different body parts both on the spot and travelling. Sharp shooting out of different body parts.

5. Exploding from a small shape, high into the air and sinking back to the floor.

Plenty of time should be allowed for the children to work on their group dances and the teacher must be prepared to help and encourage the children in their own ideas giving her own suggestions only where necessary. Percussion instruments suitable for accompanying the four fireworks are:

1. Rocket—a sharp, loud bang on the tambour for shooting up followed by a gentle tapping with the stick on the rim as the firework falls and dies away.

2. Rip-rap—the sharp, sudden sound of the castanets.

3. Catherine wheel—a tambourine shaken continuously, perhaps with crescendo and de-crescendo of sound as the movement rises and falls.

4. Roman candle—a single beat on a large triangle or cymbal followed by a gentle, vibratory sound as the movement dies away. Use a padded stick.

These accompaniments are only suggestions for the teacher for use in the movement training. The children will enjoy finding their own accompaniment for their group dances and will do so quite adequately with sounds and words if no percussion instruments are available.

WITCHES' DANCE

Stimulus: A small dramatic idea. A group of children discover a witches' coven in the woods. They are trying to get nearer to the witches without being seen when one child falls and cries out. The witches turn and see the children and cast a spell over them in their anger. They then dance triumphantly around their cauldrons. In their hurry to cast a spell on the children they overlooked the child who had fallen. She gets up and touches the child nearest to her. To her surprise it breaks the spell, so quickly and quietly she touches all the children. Together they creep up behind the witches and, with a big push, push the witches into their own cauldrons.

Music: *Witches, wizards, sorcerers and alchemists.* H.M.V. Listen Move and Dance No. 4 Electronic sound pictures and moving percussion (L.P.).

I have just given here the outline of an idea and suggested music that might be suitable. Children enjoy working on this theme and it affords excellent opportunities for a link with the classroom. The children can write their own stories and poems about witches and perhaps even make up their own spells that can be used in the dance. They will also enjoy making masks in art and craft.

CONCLUSION

Obviously there are many more suggestions I could make but I hope that some of these ideas will have been of help to the teacher, not only in the dance lesson itself but also in work carried out in the classroom.

It is important with younger children to explore as wide a variety of stimuli as possible in order to widen their experience. The suggestions given in Chapter III are by no means the only ones. New ideas and new media are within our grasp every day if we have eyes to see them and the desire to use them. From one idea, other ideas will always grow.

The suggested lessons are intended as a framework on which the teacher should build, keeping firmly in her mind the needs of her own class. She must be flexible yet clear in giving help to her children and must remember that the dance lesson is not a time for imposing her own suggestions upon the children. It is a time of opportunity when children can experiment in creativity at their own level and share their experiences with others.

I hope that this book will prove to be of use to many teachers who will take it as a guide to progression in movement and will also find within it something to stimulate their own imaginations.

LIST OF PERCUSSION INSTRUMENTS AND MODES OF PLAYING

TAMBOURINE	(1) Shaking
	(2) Banging
	(3) Scraping
TAMBOUR (drum)	(1) Beating with fingers on the skin.
	(2) Beating with a hard stick.
	(3) Beating with a soft stick.
	(4) Beating with the stick on the metal rim.
	(5) Played with a wire brush.
WOODEN BLOCKS	(1) Beating with a hard stick.
	(2) Banging two wooden blocks together.
GONGS & CYMBALS	(1) Resounding sound, hit with a beater.
	(2) Sound deadened by using the hand.
	(3) Rolls made with padded sticks.
	(4) Two cymbals hit together.
CASTANETS (clappers)	(1) Short, sharp movements of the wrist.
	(2) Vibratory movement of the wrist for continuous sound.
CHINESE BELLS	(1) One tapped against the other to produce an echoing sound.
	(2) One vibrating against the other.
MARACAS	(1) Continuous shaking.
	(2) Jerking of wrist to produce a sharper sound.
CHIME BARS	(1) Continuous rolling sound by using the beater on one note.
	(2) Using several notes to being making a melody.
	(3) Roll effect by drawing the beater across several notes.

(4) Continuous beating sound on one note.

Rhythmic patterns can be achieved by either (a) combining several ways of playing one instrument, or (b) combining the sounds made on several different instruments.

SOME SUGGESTED POEMS FOR MOVEMENT

"Small Creatures," by Douglas Fraser

Small creatures go
Their secret ways
In woods and fields and ditches;
We little know
How pass their days
Or guess the teeming riches
Concealed about
A patch of heath,
A marsh, a dune, a clearing.
Some peeping out,
Some safe beneath,
Some glimpsed while disappearing.
While rabbits hop
And weasels glide
And mice dart here and yonder,
Frogs leap and flop,
Snails stretch and slide
And hedgehogs like to wander.
Men fight a foe,
Pursue a craze,
Or plan some new invention:
Small creatures go
Their secret ways
And pay us scant attention.

"My Cat Jeoffry," from "Rejoice in the Lamb"
by Christopher Smart

For I will consider my cat Jeoffry,
For he is the servant of the living God
    duly and daily serving him.

For at the first glance of the glory of God
    in the East he worships in his way.
For is this done by wreathing his body seven
    times round with elegant quickness.

For having done duty and received blessings he
    begins to consider himself.
For this he performs in ten degrees.
For first he looks upon his forepaws to see if they are clear.
For secondly he kicks up behind to clear away there.
For thirdly he works it upon stretch with the forepaws extended.
For fourthly he sharpens his claws by wood.
For fifthly he washes himself.
For sixthly he rolls upon his wash.
For seventhly he fleas himself, that he may not be interrupted
    upon the beat.
For eighthly he rubs himself upon a post.
For ninthly he looks up for instructions.
For tenthly he goes in quest of food.
For having considered God and himself he will consider his
    neighbour.

"In the Swing," by Charlotte Druitt Cole

Fairies! Swing me to and fro!
Send me very high,
Till my toe-tips touch the clouds
Floating in the sky!

Fairies! Swing me down again,
Swing me deep and low,
Till I see the dewlit nooks
Where the goblins go.

Come and swing me fairies all!
Swing with might and main,
Swing me off to fairyland!
Swing me home again.

"By the Sea," by Leonard Clark

The tide is out to-day,
Busy children play
Games with shells and sand
Fish where rock pools stand
In shadow, half asleep,
Until the waters creep
Along the glistering land
To fill the bay.

The tide is in to-day,
The sand has gone away.
Now breakers pound the shore,
The rising waters pour
Into the hollow caves
Their never-ending waves
And loud and louder roar
With lashing spray.

"Raindrops" (Anon)

Softly the rain goes pitter-patter,
Softly the rain comes falling down.
Hark to the people who hurry by:
Raindrops are footsteps from out the sky!
Softly the rain goes pitter-patter,
Softly the rain comes falling down.

"How Creatures Move" (Anon)

The lion walks on padded paws,
The squirrel leaps from limb to limb,
While flies can crawl straight up a wall,
And seals can dive and swim.
The worm, he wiggles all around,
The monkey swings by his tail,
And birds may hop upon the ground,
Or spread their wings and sail.
But boys and girls have much more fun:
They leap and dance
And walk and run.

"Slowly," by James Reeves

Slowly the tide creeps up the sand,
Slowly the shadows cross the land,
Slowly the cart-horse pulls his mile,
Slowly the old man mounts the stile.

Slowly the hands move round the clock,
Slowly the dew dries on the dock.
Slow is the snail—but slowest of all
The green moss spreads on the old brick wall.

"A finger play for a snowy day" (Anon)

This is how snowflakes play about,
Up in cloudland they dance in and out.

This is how they whirl down the street,
Powdering everybody they meet.

This is how they come fluttering down,
Whitening the roads, the fields and the town.

This is how snowflakes cover the trees,
Each branch and twig bends in the breeze.

This is how snowflakes blow in a heap,
Looking just like fleecy sheep.

This is how they cover the ground,
Cover it thickly, with never a sound.

This is how people shiver and shake,
On a snowy morning when first they awake.

This is how snowflakes melt away,
When the sun sends out his beams to play.

Appendix III

SUGGESTED MUSIC SUITABLE FOR DANCE

A. EDUCATIONAL RECORDINGS

1. Listen, Move and Dance No. 1 (H.M.V. 7EG 8727)
   (Music for quick and light, and quick and strong movement)
2. Listen, Move and Dance No. 2 (H.M.V. 7EG 8728)
   (Music for slow and light, and slow and strong movement)
3. Listen and Move 1-8 (Macdonald and Evans. Green Label)
4. Music for dance: Series A 1-3
   Series B 1-2 (Macdonald and Evans)
5. Modern Dance: 1-4 (Macdonald and Evans. Red Label)
6. A Pageant of Dances 1 & 2 (Macdonald and Evans. Blue Label)
7. Listen, Move and Dance No. 4 (H.M.V. CLP 3531)
   Side 1 Moving Percussion
   Side 2 Electronic Sound Pictures
8. Stories for Movement Series (Decca PLP 1112-7)

B. SOUND EFFECTS

Castle Recordings—a series of extended play records by H.M.V.
   (Including police sirens, trains, breaking glass, childrens'
   noises, wind, sea, storms, ghosts. etc.)

C. LIGHT ORCHESTRAL AND POPULAR TUNES

The Music of Leroy Anderson (L.P. Mono AH 118)
The Shadows' Greatest Hits (L.P. 3CX 1522)
Herb Alpert and the Tijuana Brass (L.P. AMLS 980)

Singles: Puppet on a string
           Coco (RCA 2087)
           Zorba's dance
           Love is blue

Une Petite Cantata
Z-Cars theme
Forgotten dreams
Toy balloons
Spanish flea

D. CLASSICAL

Composer	*Title*
Arnold	English Dances 1–8 (ECS 646)
Bartòk	For Children (TV 4159)
Brahms	Hungarian Dances (SXL 6389)
Borodin	Polovtsian Dances (ASD 2345)
Britten	Four Sea Interludes (SAX 2555)
Chopin	Preludes, Nocturnes and Mazurkas (RB 16110, SB 6731–2, SB 6702–4)
Copland	Appalachian Spring (72872)
Delibes	Coppélia (SET 371–2)
Dukas	The Sorcerer's Apprentice (SDD 109)
De Falla	Ritual Fire Dance (TU 34248)
Dvořák	Slavonic dances (ECS 632)
Françaix	Divertimento (ASD 2506)
Grieg	Peer Gynt Suites 1 and 2 (6580–056)
„	Norwegian Dances (ASD 2773)
„	Lyric Suite (ASD 2773)
„	Holberg Suite (SXLP 20058)
Holst	The Planets—Suite (ASD 2301)
Inghelbrecht	La Nursery
Kabalevsky	The Comedians—Suite (SRV 207SD)
Mozart	Four German Dances (SXL 6131)
Massanet	Le Cid (SDD 139)
Mendelssohn	A Midsummer Night's Dream (SDD 159)
„	Fingal's Cave (2530 126)
Mompou	Scènes D'Enfant
Mussorgsky	Night on the Bare Mountain (6580 053)
„	Pictures at an Exhibition (SXL 6328)
Offenbach	Orpheus in the Underworld (CSO 1316)
Orff	Music For Children Vols. 1 and 2
Poulenc	Sonata

Prokofiev	Children's Suite (STGBY 601)
Ravel	Bolero (SXL 6065)
"	Habanera (SDD 214)
Rachmaninov	Variations on a Theme of **Paganini** (LSB 4011/3)
Rimsky-Korsakov	Scheherezade (SLPM 139022)
Saint-Saëns	Carnival of the Animals (CSD 1624)
"	Danse Macabre (72740)
Schumann	Carnaval (SB 6547)
"	Scenes of Childhood (SB 6547)
Stravinsky	Firebird—Ballet Suite (72046)
"	Rite of Spring (72054)
Tchaikovsky	Humoresque
Wagner	The Ride of the Valkyries (SET 390)
Walton	Facade (ECS 560)
"	Music for Children (SRCS 50)

E. MISCELLANEOUS

Six Short Pieces for Children (H.M.V.)
Tunes for Children Vols. 1 and 2 (7EG 8575/6)
Popular Classics for Spanish Guitar—Julian Bream (RB 6593)
An Andres Segovia Programme (AXTL 1060)
The World Of Charlie Kunz (PA 15)
Musical Zoo (H.M.V. 7EG 126)

F. TAPE RECORDINGS

The Music Box
Tape No. 1
  1. Walking—relaxed
  2. Running—change of direction
  3. Skipping—lively
  4. Step, hop rhythm
  5. Step, swing on spot and travelling
  6. Trotting
  7. Galloping—energetic
  8. Lilting—slow gestures
  9. Long running steps—leaps
 10. Run and leap
 11. Syncopated rhythm

12. Free expression of any of the above
13. Wringing
14. Floating
15. Pressing
16. Gliding
17. Punching
18. Dabbing
19. Slashing
20. Flicking
21. Moods. War and peace or hell and heaven

Tape No. 2

1. Walking
2. Running
3. Skipping
4. Step, hop
5. Trotting
6. Galloping
7. Syncopation
8. Wringing
9. Floating
10. Pressing
11. Gliding
12. Punching
13. Dabbing
14. Slashing
15. Flicking

The Sea

16. Dawn over the sea
17. The waves
18. Children on the beach
19. Punch and Judy
20. Storm
21. Calm after the storm
22. Hornpipe

INDEX

107

Details of
some other publications available from
Northcote House on related subjects can be found
on the following pages.

For a full list of
titles and prices write for the FREE
Northcote House Dance Books catalogue, available from:
Department D1, Northcote House Publishers Ltd.,
Plymbridge House, Estover Road, Plymouth PL6 7PZ,
United Kingdom.

Tel: (0752) 705251. Fax: (0752) 777603.

Creative Dance in the Primary School
Joan Russell

This popular large-format paperback illustrates how Laban's creative
and technical ideas can be imaginatively used in the primary school
environment. The author discusses the various ways in which the ideas
of dance can be presented to children, and follows basic theoretical
ideas through specimen lessons for 5 to 11 year olds.
*112pp, 246 × 186mm. Illustrated. £7.95 paperback.
0 7463 0359 9.*

Creative Dance for Boys
Jean Carroll & Peter Lofthouse

For many years teachers have conducted successful work in creative
movement with mixed primary school classes but development has been
limited by suspicion that creative dance is not suitable for older boys
and men. Fortunately the situation is fast improving and this
large-format book has been designed specifically for work with
boys.
72pp, 255 × 188mm. £5.95 hardback. 0 7121 0318 X.

Dance and Movement in the Primary School
A Cross-Curricular Approach to Lesson Planning

This book has been specially written to meet the needs of the
non-specialist class teacher required to teach physical education as a
foundation subject of the National Curriculum. Emphasis is laid upon
lesson-planning that encourages the development of a cross-curricular
approach, introducing the teacher to a variety of topics that form
links with both the core and foundation subjects of the National
Curriculum.
128pp, 215 × 135mm. £7.95 paperback. 0 7463 0631 8.

Dictionary of Kinetography Laban
Albrecht Knust

This large-format reference book enables kinetographers—those who use
Laban's movement and dance notation—to look up the rules and/or
symbols of the system. It can also be used as a textbook by students
unable to attend a full-time course. Volume 1 comprises the text and
Volume 2 the examples. "One of the most important landmarks in the
history of human movement studies... Beautifully produced and a joy
to use..." *British Journal of Physical Education.*
616pp (2 vols), 246 × 189mm. £35.00 set hardback. 0 7121 0416 X.

Effort
Rudolf Laban & F. C. Lawrence

This handbook will be of great value to all connected with training in either mental or manual work, its main theme being the productive control of effort in industry. The methods described improve the analysis of effort, and open up increased enjoyment of work through awareness of its rhythmic character.
112pp, 216 × 135mm. £5.50 paperback. 0 7121 0534 4.

Laban's Principles of Dance and Movement Notation
Rudolf Laban

In this standard large-format work, the author gives a comprehensive explanation of his system of movement notation, which has proved to be of such great value to dance instructors, work study engineers and all movement specialists. The latest edition has been annotated by Roderyk Lange to take account of recent developments.
80pp, 186 × 123mm, £6.95 hardback. 0 7121 1648 6.

A Life for Dance
Rudolf Laban
Translated and annotated by Lisa Ullmann

This translation of Laban's reminiscences about his early life and pioneering work up to the early 1930s tells of the experiences and thoughts which influenced him, and contributed to his extraordinary inner vision of dance. The reader cannot fail to sense the freshness and excitement in dance that filled his life in these formative years.
208pp, 216 × 138mm. £6.95 hardback. 0 7121 1231 6.

Listen and Move

This recording is the result of a careful selection of the best and most successful of the original Listen and Move series of eight 7″ records. The series was devised to help teachers of movement and dance put into practice the important principle of creativity and to provide a sound basis from which the teaching of creative dance can begin. Beginning with pieces suitable for infants and juniors and leading on to music appropriate for more senior pupils this recording forms the ideal basis for a dance library.
12″ record and guide. £5.95 + VAT 0 7121 8009 5.

The Mastery of Movement
Rudolf Laban: revised by Lisa Ullman

This is the fifth edition of Laban's important work on the theory and interpretation of human movement for dance and the stage, first published in 1950, subsequently revised by Lisa Ullman and now containing a new Preface by his son Roland Laban. Newly available, the book is a standard text for students and teachers and meets the need for greater access to the work of this remarkable German pioneer whose work has come to be widely recognised by teachers today. Illustrated.
208pp, 245 × 187mm. £8.95 paperback. 0 7463 0527 3.

Modern Educational Dance
Rudolf Laban: revised by Lisa Ullman

Since it first appeared in 1948 this book has established itself through successive reprints and new editions as a standard introduction to the study of modern educational dance. In addition to introducing the rudiments of a free dance technique, and the principles of movement observation, the book describes 16 themes designed for different age-groups, and linked to the progressive unfolding of movement experience in the growing child. Including Lisa Ullman's extensive revisions and additional material, and a new preface by Roland Laban, this new fourth edition will be welcomed by all those teachers and students today who base their work on Laban's ideas.
160pp, 186 × 120mm. £6.95 paperback. 0 7463 0528 1.

Movement and Dance Education
A Guide for the Primary and Middle School Teacher
Marion North

Illustrated throughout with photographs, this book provides the in-service or student teacher with clear and practical guidance to this whole larger field of 'movement education' and its considerable potential for child development and assessment. Complete with a set of compositions (story outlines, rituals, mimes and dramas) which the teacher can use as a basis for work with young children.
208pp, 215 × 135mm. £9.95 paperback. 0 7463 0534 6.

Music for Dance Series

The records in **Series B** were composed by John Dalby, well known for his compositions for dance. They were planned by Valerie Preston-Dunlop then director of the Beechmont Movement Study Centre, to accompany her booklets *Readers in Kinetography Laban*,

although the music is designed to be used independently of the *Readers to* accompany dance or stimulate creative movement. The records have between three and five bands on each side and a variety of time signatures, tempi and dynamics. Each piece is about one minute long. The number of bars, time signature and phrasing of each piece are given on the sleeve of each record.
Record B1—0 7121 8401 5. Record B2—0 7121 8402 3.
Each record, 45 rpm, £3.50 + VAT.

A Pageant of Dances

Ideally suited for senior children, students and recreative groups, this recording is intended both to awaken spontaneous movement, and to encourage dance composition. The music was composed and conducted by John Dalby for the pageant *The Journey of Soy*, written by Carl Huson and directed by Norman Ayrton with choreography by Geraldine Stephenson.
12" record and guide. £5.95 + VAT 0 7121 8203 9.

Personality Assessment through Movement
Marion North

Our personalities are clearly revealed to the trained and sensitive observer through the 'shadow' movements and attitudes of the body—those fleeting body-language signs that express inner thoughts and feelings. First published in 1972 and reprinted, this book has become an established text of theory and practice for the serious student of body movement, for educational psychologists, teachers, therapists, counsellors and others professionally concerned with human behaviour and development. Dr Marion North is Director of the Laban Centre for Dance and Movement, University of London Goldsmiths' College.
314pp, 215 × 135mm. £12.50 paperback. 0 7463 0529 X.

Practical Kinetography Laban
Valerie Preston-Dunlop

A practical introduction to Laban's system of movement notation, it provides a step-by-step guide for students and student-teachers of movement, with numerous examples of notation of creative movement, dance, athletics, gymnastics and industrial activities.
224pp, 216 × 138mm. £7.50 hardback. 0 7121 1609 5.

Relaxation in Movement
Dora Bullivant

Perhaps more than ever before, people are aspiring to a more satisfactory way of life; this book provides one possible path to follow. The author demonstrates how, through gentle, almost effortless movement, simple and undemanding exercises, relaxation and a sense of peace and positive well-being can be achieved.
32pp, 254 × 137mm. £4.95 paperback. 0 7121 1863 2.

A Ring-o'-Roses
Poems for Dance and Movement
Wendy Slater

A charming and original anthology for young children, Wendy Slater's new thematically arranged book of verses for dance and movement has a wonderfully magical quality. Using a delightfully free style of writing, her creative use of words—and the *sounds* of words—will quickly capture the imagination of young children, exploring the world around them in words, images and dance. Teachers and parents will find *A Ring-o'-Roses* a rich and refreshingly original source of inspiration for child-based activities, and through the use of language the children themselves will discover the magical potential of language and movement.
64pp, 215 × 135mm. £6.95 paperback. 0 7463 0525 7.